BULLOCKS CYCLES, Ltd.

FRANK P. SELTH, MANAGER.

Let Him do His Messages on a

BULLOCK

CYCLE

12 MONTHS' INSURANCE

All Cycles Built in Our Own Factory.   No Piece Work.
WE TAKE USED CYCLES IN PART PAYMENT OF NEW ONES.

From £8/10/- — 20/- DEPOSIT and 6d. PER DAY

EASY TO RIDE.   EASY TO PAY.
Electric Battery Head and Tail Light Fitted to all Cycles.

UP TO QUALITY — NOT DOWN TO PRICE.

OPEN FRIDAY NIGHT.

79 PIRIE STREET.

— PROGRESSIVE ADELAIDE —

An Early Scene in Adelaide   Near the Centre of the City

CONTRAST THIS WITH THE PHOTO ON OPPOSITE PAGE

The building shown is being offered for sale to facilitate distribution of family interests

From the time when this site was an aboriginal camping ground, constant development has taken place making it now one of the best in the city

CAN YOU VISUALISE THE INCREMENT IN VALUES AS THE YEARS PASS?

It is impossible to foretell, but it must be considerable for such a well-situated site. The most sure and secure investment offering is a well-located property in our growing city.

The building being offered provides excellent opportunities for safe investment.

Centrally situated—extensive office accommodation—fine show rooms—three strongrooms—complete lavatory accommodation—goods and passenger lifts—four tennis courts on roof—massive reinforced concrete construction.

The building is in the heart of the City, being about 150 yards from G.P.O., and adjacent to Central Market, Tivoli Theatre, Government Offices, Town Hall, Law Courts, and City Churches. It is within a few minutes of Rundle and King William Streets and the leading business houses.
This investment should appeal to attorneys representing British capitalists as the exchange position makes it particularly attractive to them.

EXCEPTIONAL TERMS CAN BE ARRANGED. FULL PARTICULARS FROM

DUNCAN BROS.

46 FRANKLIN STREET, ADELAIDE, S.A.

CITY STREETS

Progressive Adelaide 75 years on

LANCE CAMPBELL has long experience of Adelaide. Born on Unley Road, he is an arts writer and multiple award-winning sports writer. He wrote *By Popular Demand* for the Adelaide Festival Centre's 25th anniversary, and *Heart of the Arts* for its 40th. He was arts editor of the Adelaide *Advertiser*, has written satirical columns for *The Adelaide Review*, and has contributed to several books, including *McLaren Vale: Trott's View*. Lance also is arts and architecture editor of *SALife* magazine. Taking *City Streets* to the streets with Mick Bradley was one of the more enjoyable diversions in Lance's professional life, a world away from typewriters and computers.

MICK BRADLEY'S work bridges the gap between documentary and fine art photography. Mick was born in London and came to Australia as a boy. His images tell stories from our lives from the 1970s on. He honed his craft as a fine art printer, darkroom operator and photographer. Mick created his own niche in the history of South Australian photography, while his work appears in books, exhibitions and collections throughout this country, in North America and in the United Kingdom. Mick Bradley died after a sudden illness in 2013.

CITY STREETS

PROGRESSIVE ADELAIDE 75 YEARS ON

Lance Campbell and Mick Bradley

Wakefield
Press

Wakefield Press
16 Rose Street, Mile End, South Australia 5031
www.wakefieldpress.com.au

First published in association with Adelaide City Council 2012
Reprinted 2012
Reprinted with revisions 2016

Designed by Liz Nicholson, designBITE
Photoshop work and image retouching by Graphic Print Group
Printed in China by Everbest Printing Investment Ltd

National Library of Australia Cataloguing-in-Publication entry

Creator: Campbell, Lance, 1949–   , author.
Title: City streets: Progressive Adelaide 75 years on / Lance Campbell and Mick Bradley.
Edition: 2nd edition.
ISBN: 978 1 74305 413 0 (hardback).
Subjects:
Historic buildings – South Australia – Adelaide – Pictorial works. Adelaide (S.A.) – History – Pictorial works.
Adelaide (S.A.) – Buildings, structures, etc. – Pictorial works.
Other Creators/Contributors: Bradley, Mick, author.
Dewey Number: 994.231

Contents

Foreword

Within Colonel Light's unchanging 'square mile' grid, the avenues, laneways and squares of Adelaide have been in constant flux since Gustav Baring made a meticulous record of the city's streetscapes in South Australia's centenary year of 1936.

This newly reprinted edition of Lance Campbell and Mick Bradley's *City Streets* tells that story of continuity and change with insight, poignancy and acute attention to detail.

It is fascinating to run one's eye from left to right of the long photographs and see what our city has kept, what we have discarded and how we have managed – with varying degrees of success – to perform makeovers.

Though the retention of buildings has helped make, for example, North Terrace the superb cultural boulevard it is today and Rundle Street an attractive food and entertainment strip, it is hard not to feel that Adelaide lost some jewels along the way – especially the magnificent Grand Central Hotel that used to stand at the corner of Rundle and Pulteney streets.

More than just an architectural survey, this book beautifully evokes the commerce and culture, the attitudes and style, of 1930s Adelaide, including through the reprinting of old advertisements.

We are reminded, for example, of retailers like Moore's and Miller Anderson, dance venues like the Palais Royal and of trades – tobacconists, saddlers and harness makers, tailors, milliners and furriers – that have disappeared or are certainly much less common today.

What is striking about the modern Adelaide captured in this book is that – even since Mick Bradley's photographs from 2011 – the city has changed a great deal more.

Adelaide Oval, for example, has been thoroughly redeveloped, the old Harris Scarfe façade is gone from Grenfell Street, and rising up from the rail yards area west of Morphett Street is a stunning biomedical precinct that includes the new Royal Adelaide Hospital.

The Government of South Australia is delighted to support the republication of *City Streets* – a book that is lovely to read now and, I hope, will serve as a basis for the writing of another chapter of Adelaide's architectural history sometime late in the 21st century.

Jay Weatherill
Premier of South Australia

Foreword

City Streets is a wonderful anthology of Adelaide's streetscapes.

The images are a great visual demonstration of how the city has grown from humble beginnings into a place of international standing. Today Adelaide is regularly acknowledged as one of the world's most liveable cities.

With its built heritage as one of its best assets, Adelaide is also a city of immense character. These snapshots in time show that many of our iconic buildings have prevailed for us to enjoy. While some others such as the South Australian Hotel unfortunately have been lost, modern masterpieces have arisen elsewhere.

Nothing is more certain than change, so it will be fascinating to see a further comparison in the decades ahead. I am sure there will be similar dramatic shifts in the way we live and work in our city. However, I am equally sure that its heritage character will continue to shine through.

City Streets: Progressive Adelaide 75 years on had its beginnings in the 2006–2010 term of Adelaide City Council, with particular support from Councillor Sandy Wilkinson. I thank the Council of the time for initiating this project, Wakefield Press and authors the late Mick Bradley and Lance Campbell for bringing it to life, and the South Australian Government for supporting its republication.

I expect you will enjoy this book. It is a beautifully presented slice of our history.

Martin Haese
Lord Mayor of Adelaide

Introduction

In 1936, the centenary year of the former colony of South Australia, printer and newspaperman Gustav Hermann Baring published *Progressive Adelaide*. The big, handsome book was a mighty achievement. Baring wanted his State to shine on its 100th birthday.

Progressive Adelaide embraced the capital city and its seaside resorts, along with South Australia's major provincial centres. By photographing the city's street fronts, Baring created a near-perfect record of the Adelaide CBD of the 1930s.

And by financing his book with advertising, he also left us with a profile of the business life of the State as South Australia carried itself out of the Great Depression.

Progressive Adelaide is the inspiration for *City Streets*. Three-quarters of a century on, the City of Adelaide and Wakefield Press recognised the enduring significance and human interest of the first book. Yet simply reprinting *Progressive Adelaide* would have heightened nostalgia, but served no particular purpose.

Adelaide is more than its past. There is its present, and its future.

So you hold the second book. *City Streets* relives Baring's pictorial exploration of the city CBD, going to the same places, taking their photos again and pausing for stories along the way. We also have allowed ourselves the liberty of extending the range of this book beyond the original's commercial boundaries into Adelaide's rich cultural dimension.

As far as we are aware, a book of this scope chronicling two eras of a capital city has never been published before.

Certain historic buildings in *Progressive Adelaide* did not survive to appear here. There will always be a lesson in that. But Adelaide remains a captivating city in its many forms. *City Streets* re-interprets the rich legacy of *Progressive Adelaide*. It might just start a trend.

GUSTAV HERMANN BARING

Gustav Hermann Baring was one of the most enterprising South Australians of his time.

In 1910 he started Baring Printers in Chesser Street in the city. In the same year he produced the penny football budget, which became the SA National Football League *Football Budget*. The *Glenelg Guardian* followed in 1912, still going strong today as the *Guardian Messenger*.

But Baring was much more than an ink and paper printer of the old school. An accomplished cellist, in 1926 he wrote *Memories of Australia* for a competition to find Australia's national anthem. He published the song, too, with its "land of the golden wattle" sentiments, and played it on his pianola.

He wrote advertising slogans. McLeay Carpets' "Buy direct and bank the difference" remains part of the South Australian vocabulary. It is in *Progressive Adelaide*. "Dobbie's Do" is more distant, but it worked for the old-time electrical, piano and sewing machine firm.

Baring was a progressive newspaper publisher. On 12 November 1919, local Adelaide lads Ross and Keith Smith set out to fly from England to Australia within 30 days. Two days later the *Adelaide Aeroplane* hit the city streets as a "free press for the people of Adelaide".

Three more editions of *Adelaide Aeroplane* came out before Ross and Keith made Darwin on 10 December. Sadly, power restrictions brought on by a coal crisis spelt the end of this radical little rag. Original columns such as "Chapter of Incidents, Fatal and Otherwise" were no more.

For all Baring's industriousness in his prime, grandson Graham Baring recalls a loveable old fellow, a little rotund man with a donut of hair, sitting in a halo of pipe smoke on his chopping log in his back yard in Ballara Street, Mile End. "It's where I do my thinking, my boy," he would say.

"Pa believed in young people," Graham Baring says. "He would tell me, 'It's the future we have to think about'." Gustav wrote slim volumes on etiquette for young men and women. If the reader should partake of a cigarette, it was best that the habit be limited to a single smoke a day.

Likewise, although he didn't personally care for liquor, Baring decreed that a young lady could have one drink.

In the German way, he had his sweets, usually potatoes and apricot jam, before the main course. This refreshed the palate for the Sunday roast, at which Baring excelled, along with baking, stewing and pickling.

He liked to argue the political toss with his neighbour across the street, the then younger Labor lion Clyde Cameron.

Mavis Lineage, one of Baring's two surviving daughters, recalls her stepmother Eleanor taking all eight Baring children off to church while Father stayed home and plucked and cooked the chook.

Descended from the Barings of Celle in Lower Saxony and distantly related to Princess Diana, Baring was born in 1879, almost certainly at Langmeil, now Tanunda. The family moved to Broken Hill, where the boy started his working life as a toffee maker.

This he did not enjoy. So he joined the *Barrier Truth*, where he became foreman-compositor.

When the family moved to South Australia, to Waymouth Street, Adelaide, Baring committed totally to his State. "He would tell us he did it all for South Australia," says Graham Baring.

"I'm here to promote South Australia" was indeed Baring's opening gambit when in 1934, aged 55, he started work on his most ambitious publishing project. *Progressive Adelaide – As It Stands To-day* took 15 months to complete in time for South Australia's centenary year of 1936.

As far as is known, Baring took the photographs for this mammoth undertaking apart from the bonus pages for regional centres such as Port Lincoln. With that workload, it is difficult to believe that he also did all the research and sold all the advertising on his own. Advertising consultant Les J. Kyte was at the same address as Baring Printers, and comes

highly commended in *Progressive Adelaide*. He is certain to have had a hand, and gets credit here.

Every one of Baring's four sons and four daughters worked for their father at some time or other. Forty women bound *Progressive Adelaide*.

Baring family lore has it that the publisher's methods of preparing the book for publication were unconventional by today's standards. If a business paid up for advertising or just for the honour of being in *Progressive Adelaide*, all was well.

If it didn't, the business's name might be removed from the photograph. Or the building might not appear at all.

Most were happy to pay, because Baring was a man of substance, an ardent networker, well known and liked in the community. He was Gustav to his clients, Hermann to his family. He brought up eight kids during the Depression after his first wife Edith died.

At his printery in Chesser Street he gave not only his own children off-cuts to use as notebooks, but their whole school as well.

Gustav Hermann Baring died in 1960, aged 81, a contented South Australian.

Les J. Kyte was a "bright spark".

Throughout his life he learnt 11 languages. During World War II he taught Japanese to the Royal Australian Air Force. Before that he worked in advertising around Adelaide, after quitting medicine because he couldn't afford the university fees.

Port Pirie-raised Kyte appears in *Progressive Adelaide*, advertising himself. "Use my brains too," he exhorts the commercial world, "to sell your goods and services." He operated out of 10 Chesser Street, home of Baring's Printery. Hermann Baring gives him more than one chance to tout his wares in the book. "When business slackens! Call Les. J. Kyte."

Kyte may or may not have taken some of the photos in *Progressive Adelaide*. His daughter Margaret Ladner, herself a printer for 45 years, confirms he had cameras. There is a strong chance that he wrote advertising slogans with, or for, Baring. After all, Kyte had a diploma in advertising, says his son Reg Kyte, a former character dancer and road racer.

What is most likely is that Kyte went through the front doors after Baring took the photos, selling advertising space to the businesses, and writing their copy. Beyond the big department stores and perhaps the banks, insurance companies and stock firms, advertising in Adelaide would have been an open field for an educated go-getter such as Kyte.

Les J. Kyte, Advertising Practitioner and Consultant, grew into Selmor Advertising Service, or SAS. "When we walked down the street Dad would often point to a building and say, 'I put those people into business'," Margaret Ladner says. "He claimed his advertising was the best."

Kyte played the piano. Whenever business slackened for him, he taught music. Advertising, too, was different then.

BARING & BRADLEY

Hermann Baring needed a buckboard and a black cloth over his head to photograph *Progressive Adelaide*. Three quarters of a century later, Mick Bradley used tripod and ladder.

Baring must have worked hard on Sunday mornings, when everyone else was at church and the city streets were clear. He would not have seen grown men in Hindley Street hide behind newspapers at the sight of a Digital SLR. Mick Bradley did.

He would not have observed a woman remove most of her clothing and wrap it around Rundle Mall's brass pigs to keep them warm in the middle of winter. Nor did Baring bump into the singer Cliff Richard leaving A Class Shoe Repairs.

Bradley did. He spent six months of a year of his working life walking the streets of Adelaide for this book, a photographic flaneur. He spent the other six months up the ladder, a watcher above the crowd.

There's a lot of time to think at the top of a ladder in a big city, waiting for a bus to move or a light to change. Baring was a good photographer, Bradley reasoned, to take all those pictures in 15 months. Even if he didn't, and Les J. Kyte helped him, Bradley still takes off his hat to Baring.

He didn't have the traffic lights, bus shelters, wires, street signs and roadworks to contend with. But although the principles of photography haven't changed in 75 years, the technology has. Baring had to correct distortions caused by photographing buildings in narrow streets "in camera", each on a single piece of 4x5 film.

He might have had the latest roll film camera with movements, such as a German Linhof Technicka. What he didn't have was Photoshop.

For all his skills, some places defeated Baring. He couldn't straighten up the Epworth Building in Pirie Street, no matter how hard he tried.

Gawler Place was a pain, for both photographers. No room to move. Baring couldn't reach the architecture, so he shot only the shopfronts. Bradley photographed everything.

The compensations far outweighed the complications, however.

Mick Bradley first came to Adelaide from the east in 1961, to what he saw as "a smaller, more manageable Sydney, with a much prettier name". A year later, when Bradley was gone again before returning, the Tavistock Hotel was torn down for the widening of Tavistock Street into Frome Street.

Like many South Australians, Bradley didn't know that – until he went to photograph the Tavistock Hotel. He thanked the gods of building preservation that the rest of the beautiful array of South Australiana heading east along Rundle Street hadn't been treated the same heartless way.

And as a documentary photographer, Bradley thanked Baring for keeping a pictorial record of the Tavistock Hotel, so he could enjoy imagining it.

Up the ladder, Bradley found himself scrutinising Adelaide's buildings more closely than your average flaneur. He marvelled at the "extensive, intricate carving and stonework on these 100-plus-year-old constructions, the expense the

original settlers were prepared to go to, their amazing commitment to the future of the State of South Australia.

"Doing this book has driven home to me the vision of our forebears, the trouble they would go to, the love and care our craftsmen and architects had, so that their buildings would stand for a significant time.

"Where people prefer to gather is where our architecture has been preserved, like the East End. Some of the 1970s facades are starting to peel off. Maybe we'll find something worthwhile behind."

Such reflections might be interrupted by "Waddaya taking fodas of?" Or an Asian visitor's "What lens you use?" Or on moving the ladder to the next location, "The boss said you were coming, told me to look after ya. Want a drink?"

In his year on the streets, Bradley shot several thousand photographs to make up the 800 in this book. As he took them, his kinship with Baring grew. "Hermann did an extraordinary job, to even conceive of the idea. It's not a common project. I haven't seen it done to any other city.

"Perhaps in another 75 years, this book will resurface and be as intriguing as Hermann's is now."

Late one afternoon in Currie Street, as Bradley was shooting his smaller, more manageable Sydney with a much prettier name, a passer-by with an Irish lilt called to him: "God bless you for photographin' the billdin's." He shook Bradley's hand, and walked on.

Someone might have said that to Hermann Baring 75 years ago. If not, someone should have.

75 YEARS ON

The State Library of South Australia, by law, has a copy of the original *Progressive Adelaide* from 1936. The Baring family has one.

City of Adelaide senior heritage architect John Greenshields found *Progressive Adelaide* in the Holdfast Bay library, which led to a photocopy for his Council. Adelaide City Councillor Sandy Wilkinson picked up an original edition in an Adelaide Hills bookshop.

Wilkinson and Greenshields saw the heritage value of *Progressive Adelaide*. In it, the streetfronts are like black and white movie stills. So the old book is, and always will be, a resource for the repair and restoration of our historic buildings.

But *Progressive Adelaide* was never meant to be a mere manual. It was a prestige publication at a prestige time.

From that, the idea began to grow: let's do it again.

The plan was to contrast Adelaide's past with its more complex present. By presenting specific locations three-quarters of a century apart, the errors of destruction across the generations would be there to see. Ideally, in the next 75 years more of our built heritage would be retained.

Yet *Progressive Adelaide* itself seemed to grow with each fresh look at it. So, it followed, did this book. Instead of shooting a selection of buildings, photographer Mick Bradley revisited every address in the original. That meant 1800 images of Adelaide's CBD eventually appeared on the computer screen at Graphic Print Group in Richmond.

For each street section, every photo had to be "stitched" together to become one big photo. Baring used scissors, glue and his own discriminating sense of location, direction and proportion. Graphic Print Group Mac operator Peter Verheyen used Photoshop.

Even after 30 years in the trade, Verheyen found himself tested. Bradley would photograph a building with an awning or a verandah. That same awning or verandah would appear in the photo of the building next door, but with a different perspective, placed at a different angle. If not corrected, Adelaide would look like a row of shacks.

The Photoshop trick was to match the perspectives every time. Anything in front of a building could cause problems – those awnings and verandahs, tables, chairs, cars, people. Light and season changes had to be considered, too. The job took hours on the Mac, then months, and sometimes it couldn't be done. So Bradley went back up his ladder with his camera.

North Terrace heading west and Rundle Street heading east are on slopes. If Peter hadn't straightened them, both streetscapes would have wandered down the page and fallen off. Don't worry, Baring did exactly the same thing, his own way.

Verheyen was very glad that his task was a square city on a grid on a plain, that it was Adelaide not Sydney. He doubts that most cities, with their undulations and street-level idiosyncrasies, could be captured as Adelaide has been captured here. Baring did, indeed, try to do a *Progressive Adelaide* on Sydney, but he appears to have retired defeated. His *Progressive Sydney* of 1938 contains only a fragment of that city's CBD. He had better luck further out with flatter Parramatta.

Designer Liz Nicholson began her career at the end of the cut and paste era. She quickly developed an appreciation of Baring's bare-hands achievement while applying the new technology to rationalise not one, but two, books. Liz also tracked down support images from the State Library of South Australia, the City Council and other sources.

"It was the master of all jigsaw puzzles to put together, to make it read well so people can navigate it," Liz said. Along the way her eyes were opened to the enjoyment of "What a beautiful city we have, with beautiful buildings still in use."

◀ The photographer and the writer at work, in what was once the front bar of the Tavistock Hotel.

Pageant of Progress, South Australia's centenary, 1936

KING WILLIAM STREET

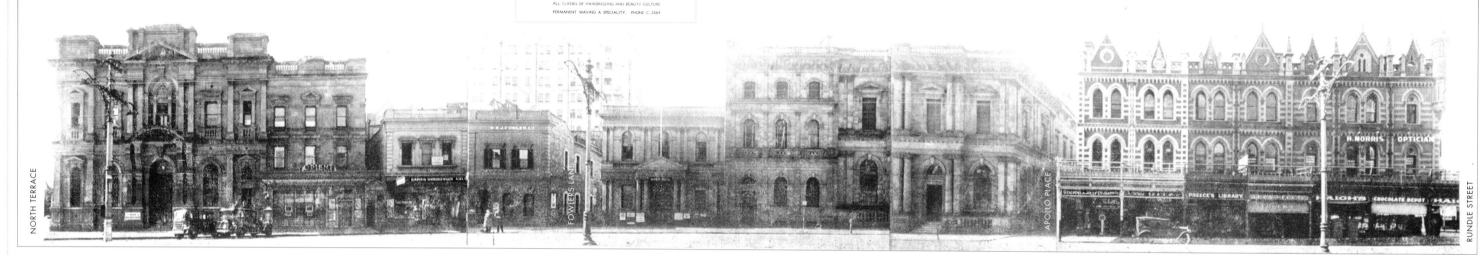

KING WILLIAM STREET (EAST SIDE), BETWEEN NORTH TERRACE AND RUNDLE MALL

FORMER BANK OF NEW SOUTH WALES
(1939–1942)

BEEHIVE CORNER BUILDING (1896)

The Bank of New South Wales building, Adelaide's finest modernist commercial building of its era, was still on the drawing boards in the centenary year. The Beehive Corner, Adelaide's Piccadilly Circus or Times Square, had been a landmark already for 90 years. It took its present liquorice allsorts form in the late 19th century, and became the city's first picture theatre. Then, like the chocolates sold there for generations, Beehive Corner was steadily devoured. It was restored 100 years after it was built, and just as well. The city would not be what it is without the Beehive Corner, where Adelaide people meet on the widest capital city main street in Australia.

WATERHOUSE CHAMBERS, Corner Rundle Street, 44 King William Street.

M.S. DURANT, Practical Watchmaker, does work of the highest class on the second floor of Waterhouse Chambers.

SHUTTLEWORTH & LETCHFORD, Licensed Land Brokers, Auctioneers and Real Estate Agents. Waterhouse Chambers. Established 1857.

GRAY'S, 56 King William Street. The only complete store for men. Founded on the principles of Truth, Style, Quality and Value—both in Mercery and Hand-Tailoring.

CHARLES WELLS & CO., Chemists, 60 King William Street, Phone: C 4717. Adelaide's Most Central Hotel. Hot and cold water in every room. Spacious Balconies. Moderate Tariff.

NOONAN'S SOUTHERN CROSS HOTEL. M.J. Noonan, Managing Director. Phone: C. 563 (2 Lines).

SANDS & MCDOUGALL PTY. LTD., 64 King William Street, Printers, Manufacturing Stationers. Established 1882.

MAIN & SON–CHEMISTS, 66 King William Street, "Accuracy"–"Service"– "Quality". "Mains for Medicine".

COVENT GARDEN RESTAURANT AND CAFE

S.O. BEILBY, Shipping and Retail Grocer and Provision Merchant, 70 King William Street, Adelaide (late Crawford's). C. 5000.

CENTRAL PROVISION STORES, King William Street, High-Class Grocers, Provision, and Tea Merchants. Phone: C. 1263 (3 lines).

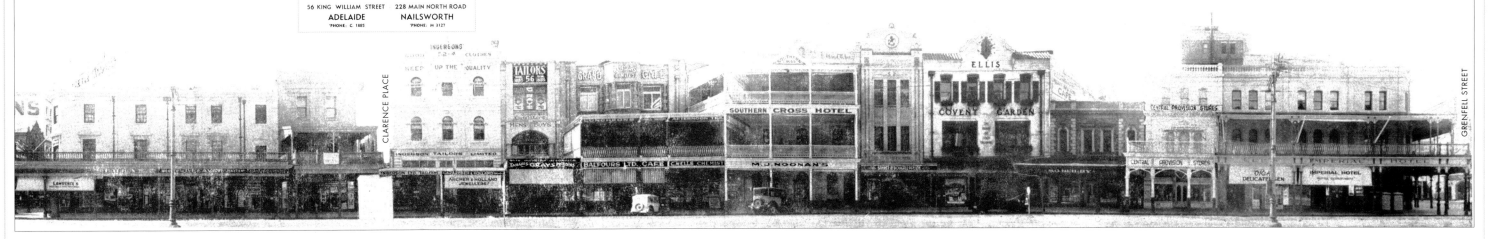

KING WILLIAM STREET (EAST SIDE), BETWEEN RUNDLE MALL AND GRENFELL STREET

FORMER WATERHOUSE CHAMBERS (1848)

SANDS & MCDOUGALL BUILDING (1881, 1933)

Directly across from the Beehive Corner, the former Waterhouse Chambers has, by South Australian standards, much antiquity. It might not be an attention seeker like its partner at the entrance to Rundle Mall, but it has stood there since the 1840s, when the famous Burra Burra copper "monster mine" paid for it. Adelaide takes the old Waterhouse Chambers for granted. Brought back to its original limewash, it would reveal itself as a graceful Regency Georgian building. Along the street, tucked in like a book on a bookshelf, the slim volume Sands & McDougall Building, or "Sands and Mac", is one of the city's great survivors. Presumably its minimal ground floor space, and consequent lower rental income, saved the loveable art deco building. In 1948 the Covent Garden Restaurant and Cafe next door went up in smoke, killing five in the kitchen and provoking a call for more ambulances. A man slid down a drainpipe to safety prompting further calls, this time for fire escapes. The modernist ex bank building there now contributes to a small yet distinctive "main drag" precinct, often overlooked despite its variety of buildings from different eras.

Technical qualification is now demanded in practically every walk of life. You can secure this readily as thousands of others have done, and are doing, Write for information now! **INTERNATIONAL CORRESPONDENCE SCHOOLS**, T. & G. Building, Adelaide.

CO-OPERATIVE BUILDING SOCIETY REG HARRIS, the noted Delicatessen Store. Hampers our speciality. Crayfish and Oysters fresh daily. **PERT & HUGHES, GENTLEMEN'S HAIRDRESSERS**, Basement. 88a King William Street. **A.J. PEEK**, Tailoring Specialist, 1st floor, Phone: C. 4929.

WOODS & SPINKSTON, Hotel Brokers and Licensed Valuers, Majestic Chambers, 100 King William Street. Hotels for sale in all parts of the State. Financial Assessment arranged. **MAJESTIC HOTEL**

WARE CHAMBERS F.L. LILLECRAPP, ESTATE AGENT, Financial Agent, 112 King William St. Phone: C. 1810. **WARD TRAINING COLLEGE** (Business). Young Ladies! Learn Quicker–Earn Sooner! Miss L.A. Ward specialises in typewriting, short-hand and book-keeping. 3rd floor. Phone: C. 2342. **BARNFIELD & GEORGE**, Real Estate, Licensed Land Brokers and Property Salesmen, Transfers,

Mortgages, Leases and All Real Property Act Documents Prepared. C. 7596. **SOUTHAM & PENDLEBURY**, Dispensing Chemists, C. 300. **TRITON INSURANCE CO. LTD.**, established 1850. E.P. Auld, Representative. Phone: C. 2218.

ARTHUR J. ROWE, CONFECTIONERY AND COOL DRINKS, 118 King William Street—first shop in row (1908).

GRENFELL STREET

CBS COURT

PIRIE STREET

KING WILLIAM STREET (EAST SIDE), BETWEEN GRENFELL STREET AND PIRIE STREET

FORMER T&G BUILDING (1925)　　　　　　　　　**COMMONWEALTH BANK BUILDING**

"More front than the T&G" is an old Australian expression acknowledging self belief. While Myer in Rundle Mall might dispute the saying's provenance, the T&G Building was the first to reach the maximum height limit of 40.2 metres, and was the best at proclaiming the city's assurance in the post Great War era. It was the first of three classical Chicago-style skyscrapers. With the CML and the first AMP Buildings, the T&G demonstrated that Adelaide had grown up. Nearby, today's precast concrete modernist Commonwealth Bank Building introduced angles to the city's grid. Inside, the bank's art for all was another initiative. Way back before the Theatre Royal, the Tivoli and long before the Festival Centre, White's Concert and Assembly Rooms, later the Majestic, were Adelaide's performing arts centre. Where the Commonwealth Bank's southern foyer is now, vaudeville and minstrel shows were all the rage.

► No one was allowed to hinder the passage of an English king, so no streets cross King William Street. They simply start up the other side with a different name.

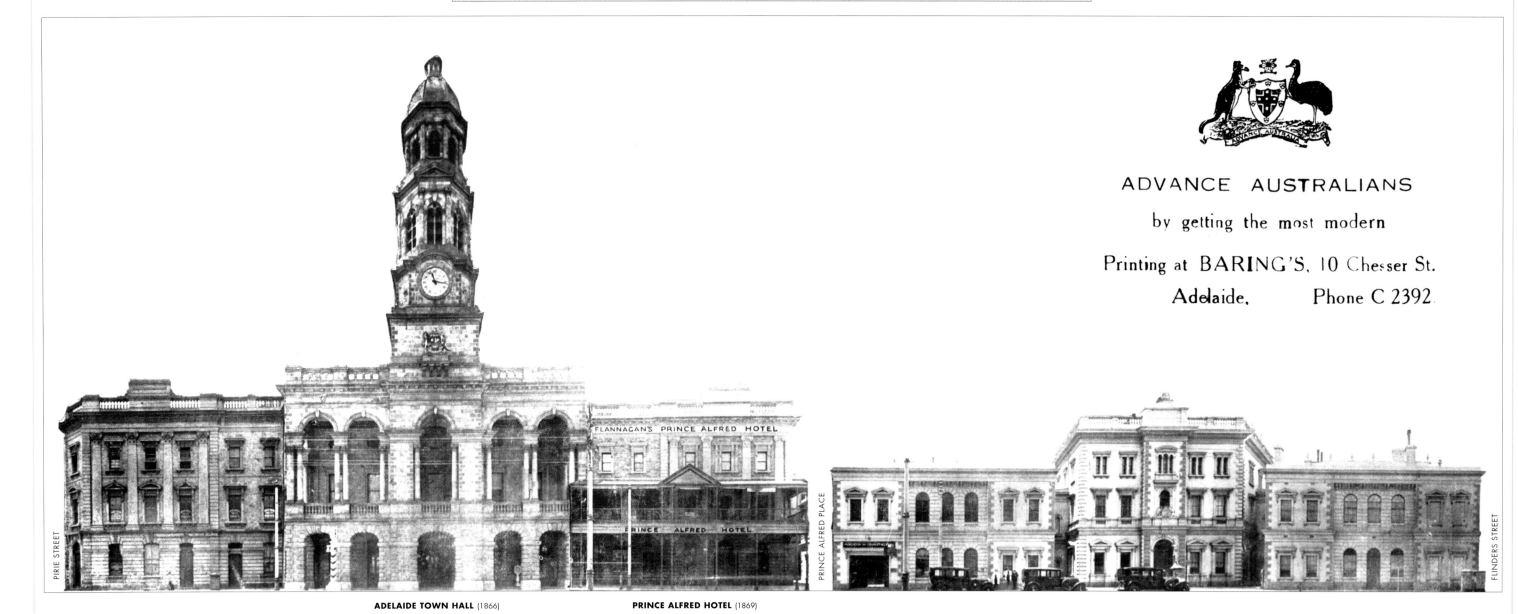

ADVANCE AUSTRALIANS

by getting the most modern

Printing at BARING'S, 10 Chesser St.
Adelaide. Phone C 2392

PIRIE STREET

FLANNAGAN'S PRINCE ALFRED HOTEL

PRINCE ALFRED HOTEL

PRINCE ALFRED PLACE

FLINDERS STREET

ADELAIDE TOWN HALL (1866)   PRINCE ALFRED HOTEL (1869)

Without dispute the biggest crowd Lord Mayor James Irwin or any other Lord Mayor of Adelaide ever pulled, or is likely to pull, gathered below the Town Hall balcony to greet The Beatles in 1964. All up 300,000 people, or one-third of the capital city's citizens, waved themselves into Fab Four folklore that day. Nowhere else in the world did such a high percentage of a population pledge itself to Beatlemania. George Harrison, the quiet Beatle, was moved to remark that the human spectacle was like the liberation of Paris. A century earlier, Adelaide's citizens showed their habitual appetite for dissent when there was talk of finishing the Town Hall in stucco. That was howled down, and Tea Tree Gully freestone did the job. Amazingly, the clock was installed only the year before Baring took this picture – 69 years after the Town Hall's Albert Tower was built. Until then, clock watchers had to look down the road to the GPO. What was the Prince Alfred Hotel now houses diligent Council workers.

FORMER TREASURY BUILDINGS (1839–1876)

The former Treasury Buildings are about as classically colonial as Adelaide can boast. Built in several stages, the first section was designed by Colonial Architect George Strickland Kingston. Inside the Flinders Street entry of what is now the Treasury Hotel, the Kingston Wall survives from the building's, and the State's, earliest days. The Cabinet Room, where successive Premiers presided over State decisions, has been preserved. More elusive is the network of tunnels rumoured to radiate from under the Treasury Buildings. There are basement vaults for gold assay, and a smelting furnace, but no passageways for crooked politicians and Treasury officials to slip away with the profits have yet been found.

FRANKLIN STREET

WAYMOUTH STREET

KING WILLIAM STREET (WEST SIDE), BETWEEN FRANKLIN STREET AND WAYMOUTH STREET

GENERAL POST OFFICE (1872)

ELECTRA HOUSE (1901)

The Anglo-Italianate GPO is finished in Glen Ewin sandstone from Tea Tree Gully, regarded as the best building sandstone in Australia until it ran out. The walls are Glen Osmond stone and the northern section Murray Bridge freestone. Most South Australians loved the GPO for more than a century. But the electronic age has reduced its beautiful main hall to a shop. The ad in *Progressive Adelaide* says, "Two old landmarks: The Criterion Hotel and Post Office". The "Cri" is gone to development, while the place next door to the north hangs in there. Just as well, too. A little bit of Florence in its appearance, Electra House is all Adelaide in its heritage. The city's first electric lift is still inside, hemp ropes intact. Once, every cable communication between Australia and the rest of the world passed through this building, declarations of war included. A group called Tuxedo Cat turns empty buildings into art spaces. In 2011 the Cat transformed loveable Electra House into a successful Adelaide Fringe venue.

KING WILLIAM STREET (WEST SIDE), BETWEEN WAYMOUTH STREET AND CURRIE STREET

AMBASSADORS HOTEL (1881)   **FORMER SAVINGS BANK OF SOUTH AUSTRALIA** (1939-1943)   **FORMER NMLA BUILDING** (1898)   **FORMER BANK OF ADELAIDE** (1880)

Behind its glass enclosed balcony, the flamboyant Ambassadors Hotel has that extra third storey that began to appear around the city in the early 1880s boom time. Originally it was the Service Club. First owner Thomas Graves was a director of the Burra Burra Mine where the copper came from, so he had it made. Next door, the Savings Bank of South Australia head office was still three years away in 1936. But it quickly became a household item. Post war, no child with a money tin shaped like the Savings Bank would live in poverty. Pennies poured through the slot. In miniature the Moderne and art deco "radio cabinet", as adults called it, was on homework desks and bedside tables all over town. A furniture store, two tailors, a shoe shop, a cash and carry and a laneway made way for the Waikerie limestone building that remains as South Australian as the Savings Bank. Two old charmers, the former NMLA Building and the original Bank of Adelaide on the corner of Currie Street, still reflect commercial Adelaide in the time of cash and chequebooks. It hasn't been easy street though. The NMLA lost ground and presence to Adelaide's tallest building, now Westpac House, behind it. When the sandstone Bank of Adelaide, later the ANZ, was extended the whole thing was painted with Boncote, which knew how to stick to cement. Seventy years on, nobody has been able to remove it.

The recently erected **COLONIAL MUTUAL LIFE ASSURANCE BUILDING** is a fine landmark on the corner of Hindley Street. **THE HOLLYWOOD HAIRDRESSING COLLEGE** is situated on the fifth floor. Phone C. 2550. **"ASTRE,"** Second Floor, for Blouses, Sports Wear, Tailored Skirts, Hand-made Lingerie, Distinctive Furs, and Pottery. **"CAPRICE"** (Miss V. Elliott), Room 501.

Millinery creator. Exclusive models moderately priced. Phone C. 2339. **"CLEOPATRA,"** Ladies' Hairdressing Salon, fifth floor (R.E. Shergis), late of Paris and Baal. Phone C. 3470. **THE IRISH LINEN SPINNING AND WEAVING CO. LTD.** – Ninth floor. manufacturers of finest linens, supplying direct to the consumers. Telegraphic and cable address: "Purelinen," Adelaide. Factory

address: Lurgan, Ireland. **P.H. PUDNEY**, Watch Repair Specialist, 1014 tenth floor, gives expert attention to all classes of watches and clocks. Phone C. 3432. **V.E.M. DATE**, High-class Tailor, is situated in this building on the eighth floor. Cut, style, and finish is guaranteed. **ETTIE PAXTON**, ninth floor, specialises in all classes of ladies' hairdressing and beauty treatment.

Phone C. 4177. **D. BEDSON**. – sixth floor, Dressmaker and Costumier. **MRS. M. FITZGERALD**, 507 fifth floor. Dressmaker and costumier. Season's frocks, coats, and costumes. Evening wear and trousseaux are specialties. Phone U 3888. **W. HARLAND'S** Toilet Salon is on the fourth floor. Permanent Waving and Resetting Specialist. Phone C. 5050. On the fifth floor is

DARELLE PRODUCTS, Ladies Hairdressing Supplies. Manufacturers of the well-known "Edmond" and "Ringletto" Permanent Waving Machines. Phone C. 2550. **J.J. BLOOMFIELD** Tailor, Hatter, and Mercer, occupies the corner shop. Specialist in all men's wear. On the second floor is the exclusive Toilet Salon of **JOAN DANIEL** (late Charles Birks), where Ladies are assured of individual

attention. Permanent Waving a specialty. Phone C. 2040. On the fourth floor, is **TOM CONWAY**, Manufacturing Jeweller. **"DOREEN"** (Miss D. Crouch), 316 third floor. Specialist in frocks, coats, costumes and renovations. **MAISON HENRI**, holder of Continental diplomas for ladies' hairdressing and beauty culture, is on the seventh floor. Expert advice. Personal supervision. Phone

C. 8800. Ladies are advised to call on **"AUTEUR"** (Eileen Dawson and Nora Isaacson), Dressmakers and Costumiers, seventh floor, before placing your order. Individual styles are assured, and fit, workmanship, and satisfaction are guaranteed. **E. GRANT WALSH**, Designer and Interior Specialist, is on the Ninth Floor. Phones C. 2781 and F 2837. **CONCRETE CONSTRUCTIONS** (S.A.) LTD.,

the builders of this modern structure are on the ninth floor of this building. Phone C. 1064. The luxurious Beauty Salon of **MISS HULDAH OSBORN** (late Chas. Birks, 8 years, and Myer's) is on the third floor of this building. Specialist in Permanent Waving and Beauty Treatments. Phone C. 3422. **MISS SKINNERS**, Dressmaker and Costumier, is also on this floor. Latest styles.

KING WILLIAM STREET (WEST SIDE), BETWEEN CURRIE STREET AND HINDLEY STREET

CURRIE STREET · *BANK OF AUSTRALASIA* · *BOWMAN BUILDINGS* · *GILBERT PLACE* · *COLONIAL MUTUAL LIFE BUILDING* · *HINDLEY STREET*

BANK OF AUSTRALASIA CHAMBERS **JACKMAN AND TRELOAR LTD.**, 2nd Floor, are Land and Estate Specialists with 35 years of reputable dealing to recommend them. Phone: C. 5617. **MISS DAVISON'S COPYING OFFICE** is on the second floor. Copying, duplicating, etc. Phone: C. 4085.

The massive **BOWMAN BUILDING** has numerous Shops & Offices, and a fine Arcade. **ARTHUR L. ATTERTON LTD.**, Tailor-Hatter-Mercer, is situated at the corner of Bowman Arcade. Phone: C. 4344. At No. 3 and 7 in the Arcade is **WALLACE**, Gent's Hairdresser & Tobacconist. **MARLBOROUGH AVIARIES**, 8 Bowman Arcade. Specialists in all kinds of Birds, Fish,

and Rockery Plants. Phone: U 4929. At No. 9 in the Arcade is **HOSKING AND JENKINS**, Booksellers and Newsagents. At No. 10 in the Arcade is **CORSET HOUSE**. Ladies' fitting by expert ensures correct support. Surgical corsets a specialty. The **BIJOU DRAPERY** is at No. 11 in the Arcade. Specialists in Ladies' Wear and Hand-Made Baby Wear and Gifts. **PREVOSTS**, the

oldest-established Ladies' Hairdressing Salon in the State is at No. 12 in the Arcade. Specialists in Tinting, Permanent Waving, and Wig-Making. **S.D. KERR**, Umbrella Dealer, occupies the first Shop in King William Street and has a large, varied stock of "rain or shine" protectors on sale. **THE SOUTH AUSTRALIAN PORTLAND CEMENT CO. LTD.** Manufacturers of the well-known

"Brighton" brand of cement. 1st floor. **PROVIDENT LIFE ASSURANCE CO.** Are also on this floor. Phone: C. 446. **THE MUSICAL BOX** is at No. 4. All the latest Music is obtainable here. Hair and moles are removed by Electrolysis at the Rooms of **MRS. FRICK**, on the 2nd floor. At 52 Gilbert Place is **H. BERRIMAN AND CO.**, Tailors. Importers of English Woollens.

INDUSTRIAL BUILDING **STERZL** Jeweller for Centenary Engagement Rings, Watches, Presents, Gifts, etc. Articles from us are Centenary quality always. Phone: C. 2971. On the 3rd floor are the massage surgeries of **CHARLES J. O'CONNOR**. **J. ANDERSON POTTER**, Seedsman and Florist, 55 King William Street. C. 1076. **DIMOND BROS.** Photographers and Art Framers. 55 King William Street. Established 50 years.

CML BUILDING See above for tenants' advertisments.

EDMUND WRIGHT HOUSE (1878)

CML BUILDING (1935–1936)

With its highly embellished intricate carving, Edmund Wright House is arguably the finest piece of stonework in Adelaide, a sculpture in itself. Sculptor John Dowie told his fellow citizens the building was a "little palace" and "the equivalent to us of a work by Palladio or Wren". Yet in the early 1970s the building very nearly became rubble. Developers planned a 19-storey office tower for the site. Premier Don Dunstan, then at the peak of his powers, found some public money, somewhere. He bought the Italianate revival former bank building for the people, and named it in memory of a colonial architect. The irony is that Wright almost certainly didn't design the building, but he made sure it happened to plan. The architect was a Victorian, and that would never do. Wright did, however, help design Parliament House and the GPO, and planted vines at Magill. The CML Building had just opened for business when Baring went around town with his Kodak. With gargoyles, lions and vultures watching over, the instant landmark synthetic stone building filled up fast. Radio station 5DN broadcast from the 12th floor. Cleopatra Ladies' Hairdressing was on the fifth, with R.E. Shergis, "late of Paris and Baal", on the tongs. Right now the CML Building is empty, and far too good to stay idle. A four-star hotel is on the cards.

HINDLEY STREET

GRESHAM PLACE

NORTH TERRACE

KING WILLIAM STREET (WEST SIDE), BETWEEN HINDLEY STREET AND NORTH TERRACE

KITHER'S BUILDING (1907)   FORMER AMP HOUSE (opened 17 July 1936)   ORIGIN ENERGY HOUSE

You wouldn't know it, but behind the square windowed frontage second down from Hindley Street is one of the city's most historic buildings. Kither's Building was the first reinforced concrete building in South Australia. As such, its heritage value is deeply embedded inside. John Monash, later General Sir John, the distinguished Australian military commander in the Great War, engineered Kither's. Before the beautiful 12-storey Sydney sandstone AMP House was replaced in its owner's affections by the big new office tower on the corner, now called Origin Energy House, it was the pride of the Australian Mutual Provident Society in South Australia. Baring caught it in the making. When finished in the middle of the State's centenary year, the AMP building captured the imagination with its grand main chamber and bronze architectural finishes. With squash courts on the roof and an entire cafeteria floor just below, the building was created to last. In its prime the old AMP building was a jewel of Adelaide. While on the outside it has been slightly tarnished by human intervention, it remains precious. Go inside the main chamber for coffee or tea, and see why. Upstairs is a tract of student accommodation – becoming a CBD staple.

Major-General Lord Dugan was Governor of South Australia from 1934 to 1939. The view from His Excellency's front gate.

ADELAIDE OVAL

The "Bodyline" Test cricket match of January 1933, pictured here, galvanised Australia and helped forge a national identity. Today Adelaide Oval is revered by cricketers and cricket-lovers alike. It has the "best bones", as they say. Acknowledged as the most attractive international cricket venue in the world, Adelaide Oval will change radically over the next few years to suit its winter purpose, Australian football. Thanks to television, the century-old heritage scoreboard is the single most identifiable symbol of South Australia. Moreton Bay fig trees and St Peter's Cathedral complete the picture.

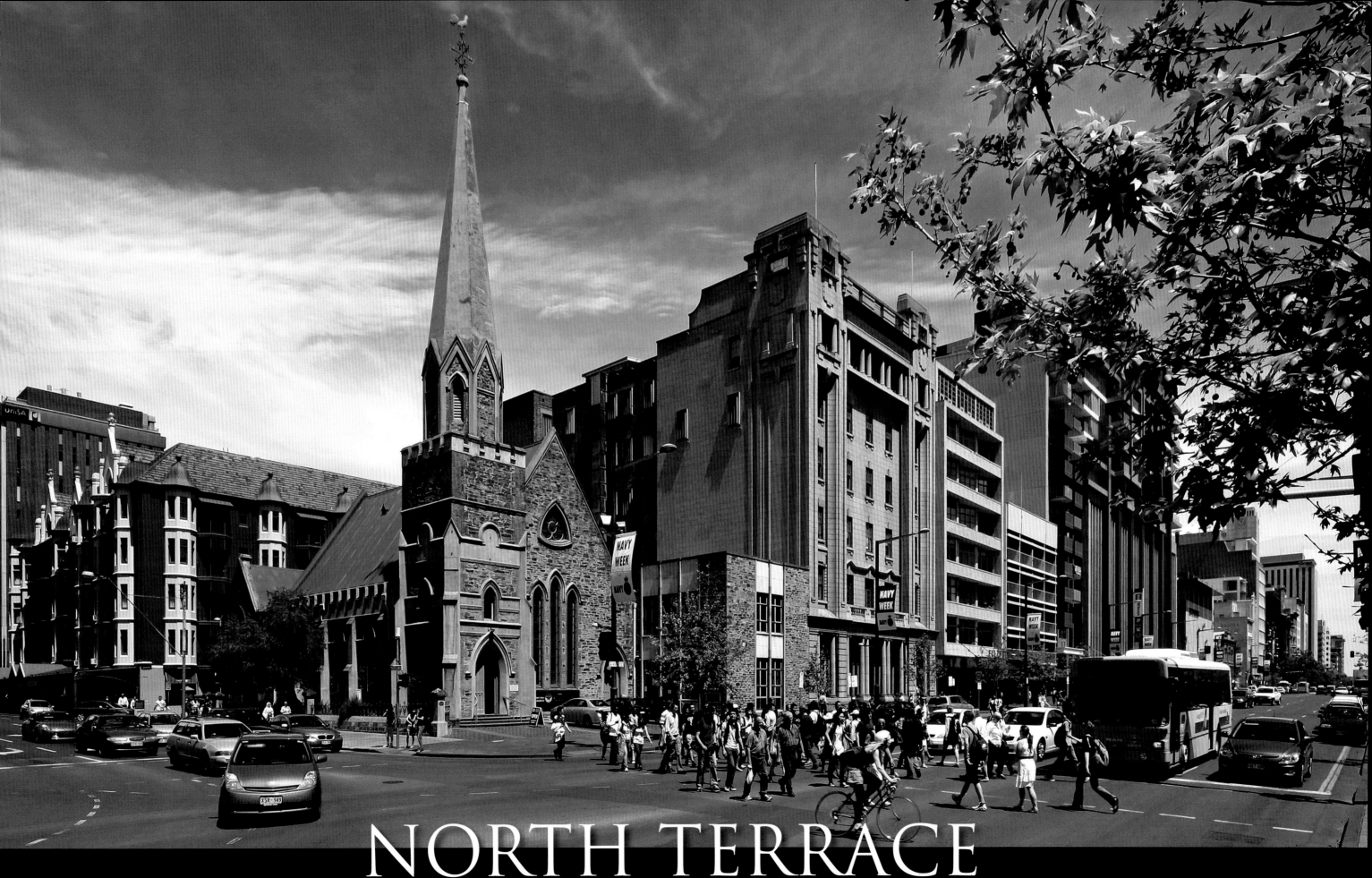

NORTH TERRACE

The Adelaide Railway Station building opened in 1928, when the steam locomotive still ruled. Its great Marble Hall is a reminder of the lost grandeur of land travel. Things have never been quite the same since the Melbourne Express and the Ghan moved to surburban Keswick.

NORTH TERRACE (NORTH SIDE), BETWEEN MORPHETT STREET BRIDGE AND STATION ROAD

In Baring's day, "All Classes of Hairdressing and Beauty Culture" were available at a large parlor run by E.J. Botten. Now, part of the railway building houses Adelaide's casino.

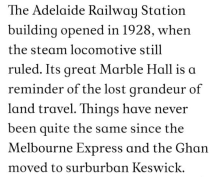

◄ Old Parliament House is a colonial charmer in limestone and red brick. It dates from 1843.

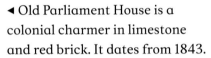

NORTH TERRACE (NORTH SIDE), BETWEEN STATION ROAD AND KING WILLIAM STREET

▶ Parliament House as we see it today was completed three years after the centenary. It had been a long haul. The first clod was turned 65 years earlier, but the pounds and pence kept running out. Newspaper magnate Sir John Langdon Bonython stumped up the cash to finish the job, then promptly died. Grand spires and domes were never added.

► With popular and government support, North Terrace has evolved into one of the most accessible urban spaces in the world. Until a better label comes along, it's our "Cultural Boulevard".

◄ Matthew Flinders, who mapped the coastline of South Australia, dressed up for the centenary.

NORTH TERRACE (NORTH SIDE)

◄ Dame Roma Mitchell, the first female Governor of an Australian State, takes a long-term view of secret men's business in the Adelaide Club across North Terrace.

▶ The Institute Building opened in 1861 as South Australia's first centre of arts, culture and science. The *Advertiser* said a theatre should be added: "A long, lofty well-ventilated room fitted with galleries and an orchestra . . . would be a real boon to the public." That would have given the State a Festival Theatre a century before it happened.

◀ The National War Memorial depicts the advent and aftermath of war through the Spirit of Duty and the Spirit of Compassion. Unveiled in 1931, it is made of Angaston and Macclesfield marble, with bronze statues. Inside are the names of every South Australian who died in the war that didn't end all wars.

▶ The alluvial soil of the Adelaide Plains is a gift to gardeners. In the decade of the centenary, North Terrace was a gallery for floral artists, its footpaths their canvases.

NORTH TERRACE (NORTH SIDE), CORNER OF KINTORE AVENUE

The State Library of South Australia documents the State. The modern glass foyer of the Catherine Helen Spence Wing contrasts with the classical Mortlock Wing, which opened in 1884 and may soon find itself converted to a museum.

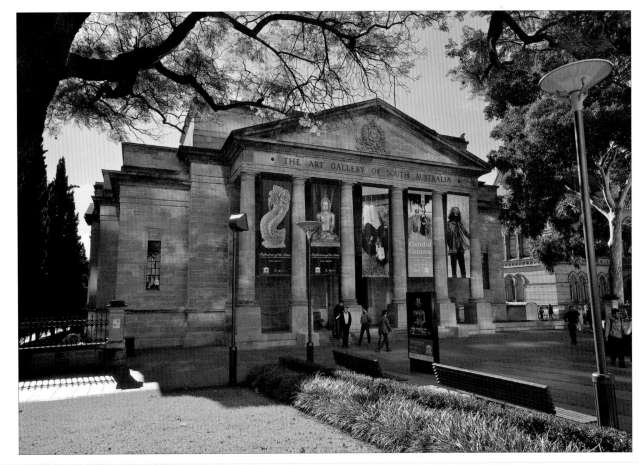

◄ The South Australian Museum is custodian of the State's natural and cultural heritage, the whale skeleton forever in a schoolchild's memory. The Museum is home to the world's largest Australian Aboriginal cultures collection, and the Waterhouse, Australia's richest natural history art prize.

► The Art Gallery of South Australia houses one of Australia's great art collections, from early colonial to dot paintings of the Western Desert. Exhibition space has been added to this beautiful building over the past century, but with 38,000 works to show, the Gallery can always do with more room. The photo here shows its centenary facade, completed in 1937.

◄ Elder Hall opened in 1900. It was threatened with extinction 40 years ago. Instead the opposite occurred, a steady internal renovation. A Casavant Freres organ was added. Today Elder Hall is a preferred concert venue, lunchtimes a specialty.

► Bonython Hall is the University of Adelaide's neo-Gothic Great Hall, scene of generations of graduation ceremonies since it opened in the centenary year. The story goes that the influential Bonython family put it there so Pulteney Street wouldn't continue through the Parklands and carve up the campus. No one has admitted anything.

NORTH TERRACE (NORTH SIDE), BETWEEN KINTORE AVENUE AND FROME STREET

◄ The Mitchell Building is the University of Adelaide's original structure. When it opened in 1882, it was the entire university. Today the Vice Chancellor occupies the sandstone Gothic building, along with legal and human resources people.

► The Brookman Building, now part of the University of South Australia, is on show again after a North Terrace upgrade. It also has been given a spring clean. The red brick Tudor revival-style building with stained glass Empire windows again defines the eastern end of an education precinct that now stretches almost to West Terrace.

The Royal Adelaide Hospital – "the RAH" to everyone – has cared for South Australians at its present site since 1856. Soon it will be replaced by another hospital at the other end of North Terrace.

The Botanic Garden to the hospital's east is of similar vintage. When the RAH goes, the garden is expected to grow into its space, so the top photo will look more like the bottom one.

EAST TERRACE

NORTH TERRACE (SOUTH SIDE), BETWEEN EAST TERRACE AND FROME STREET

BOTANIC HOTEL (1877)

BOTANIC CHAMBERS (1877)

Baring raced along what was then an exclusive mainly residential part of Adelaide. Not much commercial activity here, no point in hanging around. Yet he could not ignore the wedding cake architecture of the Botanic Hotel, one of Adelaide's distinguishing landmarks. The Botanic on the corner of East Terrace is somewhere in the mind's eye – it is the first building most people see after visiting family or friends at the Royal Adelaide Hospital. It also makes the perfect North Terrace bookend with another spectacular pub, the Newmarket across town on West Terrace. Adjacent and reflecting the same style, the very English Botanic Chambers terraces were among Adelaide's earliest prestige addresses. With their basements, the terrace houses could be in Knightsbridge, London. Doctors used them as consulting rooms, and town houses.

ANNEAR AND HARRIS (late Gawler Place Car Exchange), 275–277 North Terrace, opposite Adelaide Hospital. USED MOTOR SALES, PARKING UNDER COVER. Petrol, Oils, etc. Open Day and Night. Phone: C. 3606.

PALAIS ROYAL

VAUGHAN PLACE

NORTH TERRACE (SOUTH SIDE), BETWEEN EAST TERRACE AND FROME STREET

AYERS HOUSE (1846, 1859)

PALAIS APARTMENTS

Sir Henry Ayers was the biggest name in South Australia for much of his life, tycoon, politician and philanthropist. His Regency-style Ayers House is the only mansion left on North Terrace, a reminder of the colonial knight's power and influence. Its interior decoration is a major attraction. In its landscaped grounds, Ayers House has been many things to South Australians – military club, restaurant, museum, function centre, film set, a nurses' home. Where the Palais Apartments are now, the Palais Royal, or Palais de Danse, attracted dancing fiends across the generations. It had a wooden floor, and was made mainly of galvanised iron, chicken wire and louvres. The great Australian entertainer Peter Allen performed there at the age of 17. As teenagers, History SA chairman Phil Broderick and Tony Murray were on their way into a concert at the Palais Royal. They asked a "funny little bloke" sitting in a small room out the back where they could find the toilet. "Man, the whole place is a toilet," was the reply. Phil and Tony had enjoyed a private audience with Bob Dylan. The following year, 1967, the Palais was turned into a parking station. Bobby might have been around the mark.

Adelaide branch of the
**GOODYEAR TYRE AND
RUBBER COMPANY**,
251 North Terrace.

MINIATURE GOLF LINKS on
the east corner of Pulteney
Street and North Terrace.

Crowds wait in Pulteney Street
and North Terrace for Father
Christmas, 1935.

PULTENEY STREET

NORTH TERRACE (SOUTH SIDE), BETWEEN FROME STREET AND PULTENEY STREET

FORMER HOUSES (1872)   HOUSE (1881)   FREEMASONS HALL (1872)

SCOTS CHURCH (1851)   KELVIN HOUSE (1926)

The slate mansard roof defines the house alongside Freemasons Hall as French Second Empire architecture. It has been a private home for imaginative city dwellers, but in the past was a guesthouse and doctors' rooms. The Chinese herbal specialist Dr Lum Yow was a tenant. He also consulted out of the pair of houses with the palm trees immediately east. In the 1920s, Dr Lum was involved in "The Lum Yow Case" in which he used herbs to treat a woman with cancer. Unhappy with the outcome, the woman asked for 5000 pounds in damages. Top lawyers were involved, and the Press had its day. An undisclosed settlement was agreed in court, Dr Lum continued his practice, then died, aged 64. He is in an impressive family plot on West Terrace. The Freemasons Hall itself is a temple to craft, almost unheard of these days. It also has a Hall of Fame, often heard of these days and considered a modern American invention. Yet this Hall of Fame was in the plans almost a century ago. It is well worth a look, along with the Great Hall at the back, all part of one of the city's most elaborate assemblages.

VERCO HOUSE (demolished 1963)

FORMER DOCTOR'S ROOMS

G&R WILLS

NORTH TERRACE (SOUTH SIDE), BETWEEN PULTENEY STREET AND GAWLER PLACE

OLD "JOHNNIES" CAR PARK   DAVID JONES   FORMER DOCTOR'S ROOMS (1901)   FORMER G&R WILLS WAREHOUSE (1870s)   TOBIN HOUSE

The old "Johnnies" car park that dominates this scene is a landmark, of sorts. With the addition of apartments on top, it attracts people to live and work in the city. On the original 1901 plans for eye surgeon Dr Mark Symonds's new consulting rooms was a small area marked "Boy". This, we can hazard a guess, was a space for a youth down on his luck who would take deliveries and run errands for the medical profession. Distinguished by its oriel window, the Gothic secular revival building is rare in Adelaide. Though dwarfed today by the rear of David Jones immediately to its left here, it is a beautiful reminder of an era when it was considered de rigueur for leading medicos to settle for nothing less as a workplace along North Terrace. Next door the former G&R Wills building had more modest ambitions. It was a warehouse. Along North Terrace, however, even warehouses had to look good, and this one does it with Italianate revival style. Another Gothic secular revival building, Tobin House, has been converted to student accommodation. Big windows let in the natural light, and with it the views across Government House to Adelaide Oval.

GAWLER CHAMBERS (1914)   QUEEN ADELAIDE CLUB (1909)   VERCO BUILDING (1912)   LIBERAL CLUB (1924)   GOLDSBOROUGH HOUSE (1935)   SHELL HOUSE (1931)   ADELAIDE CLUB (1864)

Phone C 1401
THE FOOT ROOMS
FOR
LADIES AND GENTLEMEN
AN EXCLUSIVE INSTITUTION FOR THE
TREATMENT OF CORNS, BUNIONS, AND
ALL FOOT TROUBLES
FIRST FLOOR
VERCO BUILDINGS
NORTH TERRACE
MISS HALSEY
FOOT SPECIALIST
SUPERFLUOUS HAIR
PERMANENTLY DESTROYED
BY
ELECTROLYSIS
ALL BRANCHES OF LADIES HAIRDRESSING AND TOILET WORK

A VIEW OF THE
WENTWORTH TEA ROOMS
LIBERAL CLUB BUILDINGS, NORTH TERRACE
'Phone C 4778

NORTH TERRACE (SOUTH SIDE), BETWEEN GAWLER PLACE AND KING WILLIAM STREET

In the roll call of South Australian history, after the Old Gum Tree there's Gawler Chambers. The South Australian Company did the colony's founding business, and built the Mayfair-style Chambers. Like many older city buildings, getting around inside is difficult by modern standards. But Gawler Chambers' heritage and visual appeal are intact, right down to the Murray Bridge granite. Next door, the Queen Adelaide Club shows the residential character of North Terrace before the skyscrapers moved in. The Queen Adelaide Club has been the comfort zone for the female Adelaide establishment for more than 100 years. Soaring six storeys a century ago, the Verco Building was the city's first skyscraper. Today, along with the Liberal Club, Goldsborough House and Shell House, it is an exterior film set of Adelaide between the world wars. To the west of Shell House, the Dry Creek stone Adelaide Club has been the bastion of the male Adelaide establishment for nearly 150 years, a place where governments were made. Today most of these buildings are facades, shadows of their former selves, at the back end of a department store. When Baring took their picture, the medical and dental professions flourished along the row. Politicians, pastoralists and industrialists made their moves there. Better an authentic reminder of our heritage than none at all.

GRESHAM HOTEL

SOUTH AUSTRALIAN HOTEL

KING WILLIAM STREET · BANK STREET · GRESHAM STREET · WOODSONS LANE · BANK STREET

NORTH TERRACE (SOUTH SIDE), BETWEEN KING WILLIAM STREET AND BANK STREET

ORIGIN ENERGY HOUSE

After 114 years, the lovely old Gresham Hotel made way in 1965 for the new AMP building, produced in the international manner and these days known as Origin Energy House. Just to the west, the South Australian Hotel, "The South", hung on for another six years. The State's epitome of colonial style was the Raffles of Adelaide, cool, shady and elegant. When Baring photographed the South, owner Louisa O'Brien greeted all guests in the foyer while legendary maitre d' Lewy Cotton checked the gentlemen's neckwear. Louisa was called the "Grand Duchess of the hotel world". Where the Duchess of The South once reigned supreme, a modern five-star hotel now does its duty.

BANK STREET

BLYTH STREET

VICTORIA STREET

NORTH TERRACE (SOUTH SIDE), BETWEEN BANK STREET AND VICTORIA STREET

STRATHMORE HOTEL (1880)   **GROSVENOR HOTEL** (1919)

With the recent neoclassical Adelaide Railway Station across the way providing one of South Australia's two international gateways in 1936, hotels both residential and convivial occurred naturally along western North Terrace. The later change of name from the rail-flavoured Terminus Hotel to the Strathmore didn't stop Adelaide's print media making it home away from work for another 50 years. It was a short walk west back past the Grosvenor to the headquarters of the *News*, where Rupert Murdoch learnt his trade. The Grosvenor was then proudly temperance and the State's largest residential hotel. Its roof is alleged to be the spot from where a radio announcer once broadcast the cricket at Adelaide Oval, 500 metres across the railway tracks and the Torrens. While room tariffs have gone up from 6/-, or 60c, a day, the original marble facade survives. The bar is now open.

HOLY TRINITY CHURCH (1838, 1880s)

The venerable Holy Trinity was in the action from the start, down near the Torrens where the drinking water was. It is the State's oldest church, with a stained glass window dating from Colonial Year One.

NORTH TERRACE VIEWS FROM MORPHETT STREET BRIDGE

Fowler's "Lion" brand was a grocery giant on both sides of Federation. Its landmark red brick factory building was completed in 1906. Later the building lost a physical side to road-widening and bridges. But as the Lion Arts Centre, it grew another life. The visual and multicultural arts flourish here, along with dance and music. Another giant, the annual Adelaide Fringe, reached critical mass "at the Lion".

-38-

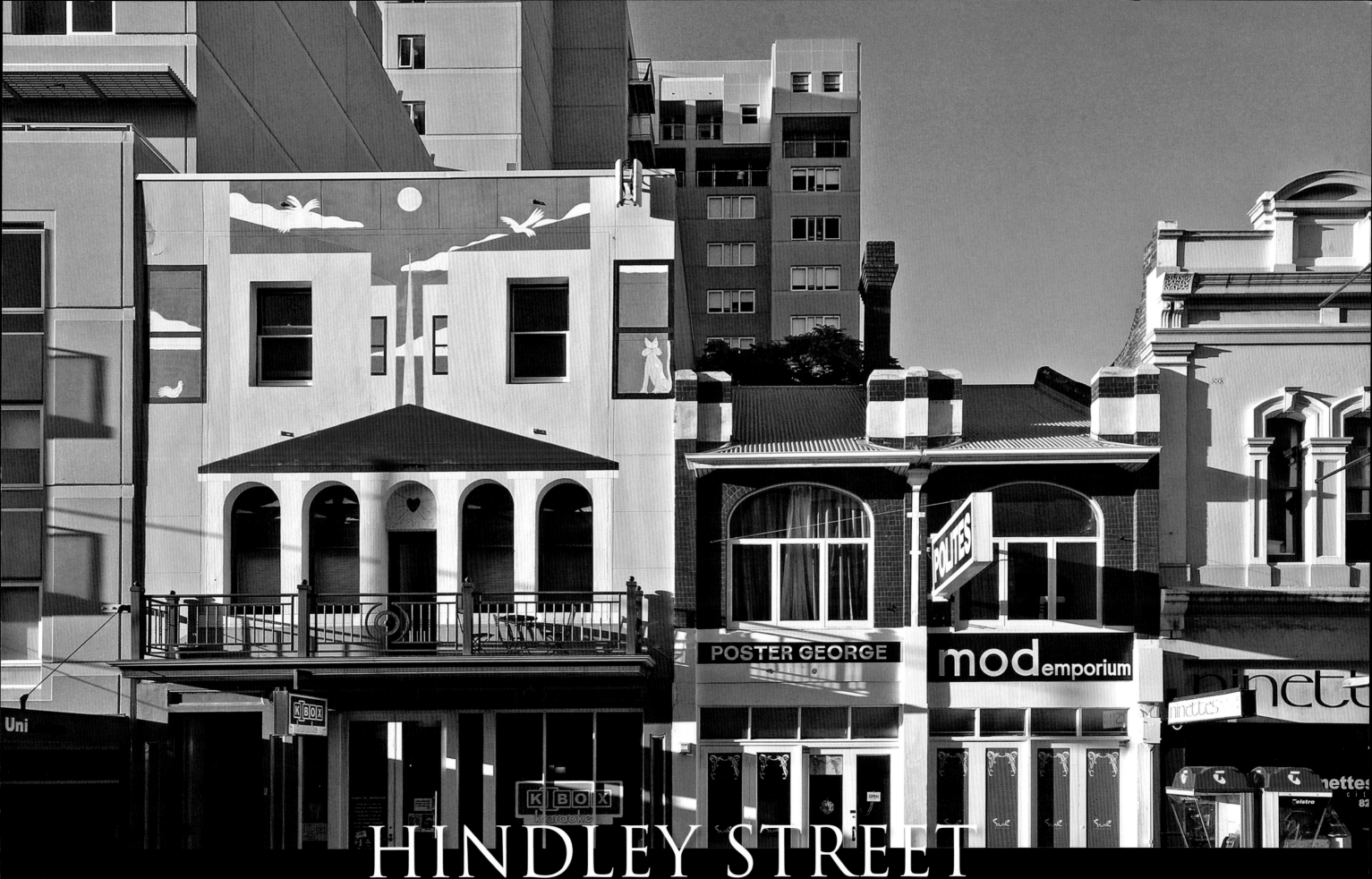

HINDLEY STREET

S.A. ALLEN & SONS, West's Coffee Palace Building. Saddlers, harness, and collar makers. Phone: C. 1179.

WEST'S COFFEE PALACE

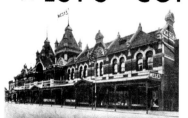

"THE HOUSE WITH A HOMELY ATMOSPHERE"

110 HINDLEY STREET, ADELAIDE

Telephone: Central 1993

CLEANLINESS	::	COMFORT
COURTESY	::	ATTENTION
SPLENDID TABLE	::	FREE GARAGE

– TARIFF –

PER DAY 8/- – – PER WEEK £2-9-0

SINGLE BEDROOM AND BREAKFAST 5/- PER DAY

Address All Letters, Telegrams, Etc. to the Manager

WEST'S COFFEE PALACE – – ADELAIDE

F. H. WEST, Proprietor

L.C. CRICKMAR Wholesale. Dress and Mantle manufacturer. Most up-to-date workroom in the city, equipped with most modern machinery. West's Coffee Palace Buildings, 106 Hindley Street Phone: C. 3388.

WEST'S COFFEE PALACE (1903)

The vista directly south from West's Coffee Palace to the Queen's Theatre off Currie Street is one of the best in the city. So what price the return, after 50 years, of the balcony in Baring's photo? West's is a South Australian landmark. Built as The Austral Stores in 1903, the ornate design was a sign of happy, optimistic times. It aligned with the sophisticated European approach, where the architecture prevailed and the businesses fitted in without dominating the landscape. West's still prevails. Its transition to coffee house was the work of the temperance movement, which would have been horrified at ensuing events there. In the 1960s the pioneering Caon Brothers established La Cantina downstairs at 108 Hindley Street, and the long-denied Adelaide public was introduced to the hedonism that good food, good wine and good company begets. La Cantina was a showbiz favourite, where Dame Margot Fonteyn would partake of a light pre-ballet salad at 5 pm, and Dame Joan Sutherland would sing an aria at 5 am. The comic Spike Milligan rang from London to book a table. With his hungry colleagues around him, the great dancer Rudolf Nureyev would consume a post-performance bottle of BYO champagne with a marinated sirloin steak by himself, then proclaim, "Now the peasants can order and eat!" Rudi's newly defected compatriot Mikhail Baryshnikov, unused to Western gin, had to be carried up the stairs by manager Paul Limpus. No one who went there ever forgot La Cantina underneath West's Coffee Palace, for the sheer first romance of it all.

VICTORIA STREET

BLYTH STREET

HINDLEY STREET (NORTH SIDE), BETWEEN VICTORIA STREET AND BANK STREET

FORMER MACROWS (1884)   PRINCES BERKELEY HOTEL (1878)   **50 HINDLEY
STREET**

In 1936 in the old Macrows "Everybody's Furnishers" store, a complete dining room suite could be loaded for home delivery from one of the city's more baroque buildings. The Princes Berkeley Hotel came to Hindley Street in 1838 via the West Parklands' Buffalo Row settlement, named after HMS *Buffalo*. It took on its present form during the 1870s building boom, and has managed to keep its Queensland cast-iron filigree-style balcony. Not long after Baring snapped it as the Black Bull, the hotel was the source of a rumour about the whereabouts of the legendary lost explorer Ludwig Leichhardt. An expedition ventured forth from the hotel to the edge of the Simpson Desert. Alas, no Ludwig. Unfortunately for Hindley Street, the impressive premises of W.T. Flint & Son, Ltd, importers, ironmongers, drapers and house furnishers, disappeared for the widening of Bank Street. Fortunately for the street, though, the building that replaced part of it had character too. With not much ground room to move, in the late 1950s a narrow modernist bank building worked its way down Bank Street. With its blue tiles and full glass curtain wall, 50 Hindley Street is another city landmark, this time on the walk to the railway station and the train home.

KEARNS BROS. & CADMAN
(With which is absorbed the business of F. Matthewman)
ADELAIDE'S LEADING AUCTIONEERS   12   BANK STREET

BANK STREET

GEO. LEWIS, Wholesale and Retail Confectioners. Our own sweets are made daily on the premises. Buy your sweets from Geo. Lewis and save money. Our own wholesale prices are incomparable. Phone: C. 3669.

L.F. ROSE, 20 Bank Street, Newsagent and Lending Library.

Latest Fiction, etc., in stock. Also this "PROGRESSIVE ADELAIDE" Photographic Directory. Convenient to Station. Parcel depot.

ARMSTRONG LIMITED, 22 Bank Street. Pianos, Players, and Music. Radio Dealers. Phone: C. 2581.

KEARNS BROS. & CADMAN, Adelaide's Leading Auctioneers,

who have absorbed the business of the late F. Matthewman. Auction Sales conducted anywhere. Regular Mart Sales held Mondays and Wednesdays. Private sales daily. These Auction Rooms are the largest in Australia. £10,000 stocks of high-grade furniture to select from. Buyers of any quantity second-hand furniture

out-right for spot cash. Licensed Land Brokers. All classes Real Estate Work undertaken. Phone: C. 1526.

MOYNHAM'S TYRE AND RUBBER STORE, 26 Bank St., for better value and service. Motor Cycle Tyres, Sports Goods, Raincoats, and Garden Hose. Phone: C. 1723.

FORMER SAVINGS BANK OF SOUTH AUSTRALIA (1958)

EAGLE HOTEL

Before the Bank Street widening, Adelaide here wears its London look. Forty years on, the Eagle Hotel self-served roast beef and salads on butcher's blocks in summer, with pots of hot soup over the fire in winter. Now the Eagle is a McDonald's. Mick Bradley stayed at this hotel when he first came to Adelaide with his family in 1971.

No matter what its times and guises, Hindley Street has its place for all South Australians. Church, media and politics began here. A few street fights, too. Before the CML Building dominated the street's eastern end corner, the horse and dray still had right of way.

THEATRE ROYAL in 1955.

WARES EXCHANGE HOTEL

GRESHAM STREET

KING WILLIAM STREET

HINDLEY STREET (NORTH SIDE), BETWEEN BANK STREET AND KING WILLIAM STREET

ROY RENE

MILLER ANDERSON

The proprietor of the Theatre Royal apparently didn't respond positively to any kind offer of international exposure, because the 1878 building doesn't appear in *Progressive Adelaide*. The theatre building went in 1962 to make way for Adelaide's first multi-level car park. A tragedy of Greek or Shakespearean proportions – take your pick. Sir Laurence Olivier played Richard III at the Theatre Royal and loved it. Next door, Miller Anderson is an upmarket interwar classical department store turned student accommodation. Alongside is an attractive mix of Edwardian and Italianate – an Adelaide building worth keeping. Across Gresham Street, where a highrise now dominates, Adelaide's oldest hotel in its original building stood until 1960. The story goes that Samuel Payne won the Exchange Hotel's 12-shilling town acre for "a bottle of rum and a song" wager on the boat on the way out. He built the pub of pine in 1839. When Baring came looking almost a century later, "the little, low-raftered rooms with their quaint pictures, where the old squatters sat smoking their fat foreign cigars and drinking their gin . . . are still the same". Strike me lucky! Harry van der Sluys was Roy Rene was Mo McCackie, born in 1891 across Hindley Street from where he stands today, looking at where the Theatre Royal used to be. Roy began his professional theatrical career there, in *Sinbad the Sailor*. He was a great vaudeville and radio comedian, Australia's funniest man, a kind of Chaplin to his country.

PEEL STREET

HINDLEY STREET (SOUTH SIDE), BETWEEN KING WILLIAM STREET AND PEEL STREET

PARINGA BUILDING   **TATTERSALLS HOTEL** (1902)   **FORMER WONDERGRAPH THEATRE**

With City Council help, the Paringa Building survived a bout of concrete cancer to live on as boutique accommodation. That's a radical usage change from the prizewinning Miss N.E. Hunt, smocking specialist, and Miss V.J. Willshire, who made winged cloth badges for the SA Harley Motorcycle Club in 1936. Tattersalls Hotel was built during a brewing boom. More than a century on, its blackwood panelled back bar evokes a past era of European elegance like no other pub in Adelaide. The bar is intact, its ambience irreplaceable. "Wait a minute, wait a minute, you ain't heard nothin' yet!" On the night of 2 March 1929 at the Wondergraph Theatre, Al Jolson's *Jazz Singer* brought the talkies to town. Entertainment in Adelaide never was the same again. When it opened in 1913, the Wondergraph was "the finest picture theatre in the Southern Hemisphere" – as each new cinema of the silent era tended to be. But the "Wonder" with its leadlight windows and amusement park architecture, made good its claims. It survived as the more sober Civic and State, and had a short new millennium life in cabaret. Now it is a convenience store.

S.O. BEILBY, Shipping and Retail Grocer and Provision Merchant, 35 Hindley Street (cr. Peel Street). Central 5707.

LEIGH STREET
Church people and Sunday school teachers are recommended to call at the **A.B.M. BOOK SHOP** (Australian Board of Missions), 22 Leigh Street, and inspect the varied stock of Bibles, Hymn, Prayer Books, Sunday School Books and Materials, Children's Books and General Literature. Country enquiries receive prompt attention. Phone C. 6379.

A. McDOUGALL'S FISHING TACKLE DEPOT, at 24 Leigh Street, is the oldest business of its kind in the State, established in 1885. All fishing requisites are obtainable here. Country orders receive prompt attention. Phone C. 7328.

The Store for Good Value! **COOK'S** "Where Men buy best". Suppliers of every clothing requirement and men's accessories, etc. at prices men are pleased to pay. Made to Measure and Ready-to-Wear Suits, Hats, Ties, Shirts, Underwear, Footware, Travelwear and Sportswear. **COOK, SON & CO.**, Men's Tailors and Complete Outfitters. 53-55 Hindley Street.

HINDLEY STREET (SOUTH SIDE), BETWEEN PEEL STREET AND CLUBHOUSE LANE

FORMER HOOPER'S FURNISHING ARCADE

The Hooper's Furnishing Arcade was only five years finished in 1936, although the furniture company itself had been on the same spot for 70 years. With its double-storey bronze window elements, the later John's Period Furniture building won its heritage listing hands down. While both firms have departed, their sense of style continues along adjacent Leigh Street, revived and alive with restaurants. It is an apt junction, because from here west to Morphett Street was where South Australia came of age as a place to dine. After World War II, slowly but deliberately the Italian migrant community brought European dining style to a meat and three veg society. The Sorrento and Pagana's led the way, then Flash Gelateria, the Black Orchid and the Desert Sands upstairs added real coffee to the ham and cheese toasted sandwich agenda, with or without tomato. When cappuccino finally reached these shores, Adelaide, in all its gustatory innocence, would queue down side streets almost as far as North Terrace in anticipation of a cup of froth.

HAINS HUNKIN LTD.
Complete House
Furnishers.

R. CASHMAN & CO.,
71 Hindley St., Watch-
makers and Jewellers.
Repairs a speciality.
Established 32 years.
Phone: 1962.

DAVID PRATT has had
lifelong experience
amongst birds and
animals, including 25
years at the Zoological
Gardens. The knowledge
gained by this experience
is at your disposal at his
BIRD AND DOG STORE,
95 Hindley Street.

CLUBHOUSE LANE

HINDLEY STREET (SOUTH SIDE), BETWEEN HOTEL GRAND CHANCELLOR AND DOG & DUCK ALE HOUSE

HOTEL GRAND CHANCELLOR

PLAZA HOTEL   ADELAIDE SYMPHONY ORCHESTRA

In 1936, Adelaide's night street of today was a busy commercial strip, where ex-zookeeper David Pratt ran his Bird and Dog Store, and K.Y. Yuen did your laundry. Heading west from the Hotel Grand Chancellor where Hains Hunkin once was, a return to some of these original shopfront elements in the public realm would add to the cultural and commercial value of the street. The centenary year came too soon for West's Cinema, which grew from a skating rink next to Pratt's Bird and Dog in 1939. Somebody had to show *Gone With the Wind*, and West's came along in the nick of time. Likewise the new Metro across the street. Both played *GWTW* until Rhett still didn't give a damn, but only West's remains. It now houses the Adelaide Symphony Orchestra.

ADELSON'S,
117 Hindley Street. Tailoring and Mercery Specialists. Our Ready-to-Wear Suits at 42/- cannot be beaten in the city.

P. GARDNER,
119 Hindley Street. Hairdresser and Tobacconist. Est. over 40 years. Cleanliness, civility, & attention.

K.Y. YUEN,
121 Hindley Street. Laundry. Suits cleaned and pressed. Prompt delivery.

HOTEL KALGOORLIE

The Kalgoorlie, today the Red Square Night Club, dates back to the first half of the 19th century. A kind of saloon-justice still prevailed more than 130 years later when women were banned from the front bar of what was then called the Mediterranean Hotel. The publican, Australian football legend Noel "Teaser" Teasdale, reasoned that West End prostitutes who worked the room lowered the tone of his establishment. The simple solution was to refuse service to all women, from "pros" to primary school teachers. Teaser believed he had brought peace to his front bar until he came up against South Australia's new Sex Discrimination Board, which advised him to let the ladies in and leave the law to the lawmen. Adelaide hospitality folklore has it that Teaser took the news like a man.

THE ROMA TAILORING (R.F. Zappia), 125 Hindley Street. Specialists in all classes of gentlemen's tailoring and ladies' costumes. All work done on the premises.

ROYAL ADMIRAL HOTEL

GLADBEAMS BUILDINGS

A. CARAPITIS, 143 Hindley Street, Hairdresser and Tobacconist. Civility and cleanliness guaranteed.

THE STAR GROCERY, 145 Hindley Street. Phone: C. 7958.

MORPHETT STREET

HINDLEY STREET (SOUTH SIDE), BETWEEN DOG & DUCK ALE HOUSE AND MORPHETT STREET

DOG & DUCK ALE HOUSE   **CACAS CHEMIST**   **JERUSALEM SHESHKABAB HOUSE**   **CRAZY HORSE REVUE**

The Dog & Duck was long the Royal Admiral, a pub since 1838, one of the first brick buildings in the street. With Cacas Chemist to the east and Jerusalem Sheshkabab House in the middle, the large Italianate Gladbeams Buildings survive along the nightlife beat, though deprived of their classical ornamentation. Heritage experts say the original character can be restored. Further to the west, another Hindley Street institution wasn't so lucky. The Star Grocery, "Importers of European goods" and manufacturers of the Star brand cigarette papers and "Stella d'Italia" tomato conserve, later moved to the corner of Morphett Street. The Star Grocery served Adelaide's migrant population and more adventurous eaters for generations. This strip has given Hindley Street its name for playing on into the night. So the Crazy Horse Revue, still dancing after 31 years, must be heritage. The city's Arab community likes to meet along here, to smoke the traditional hookahs.

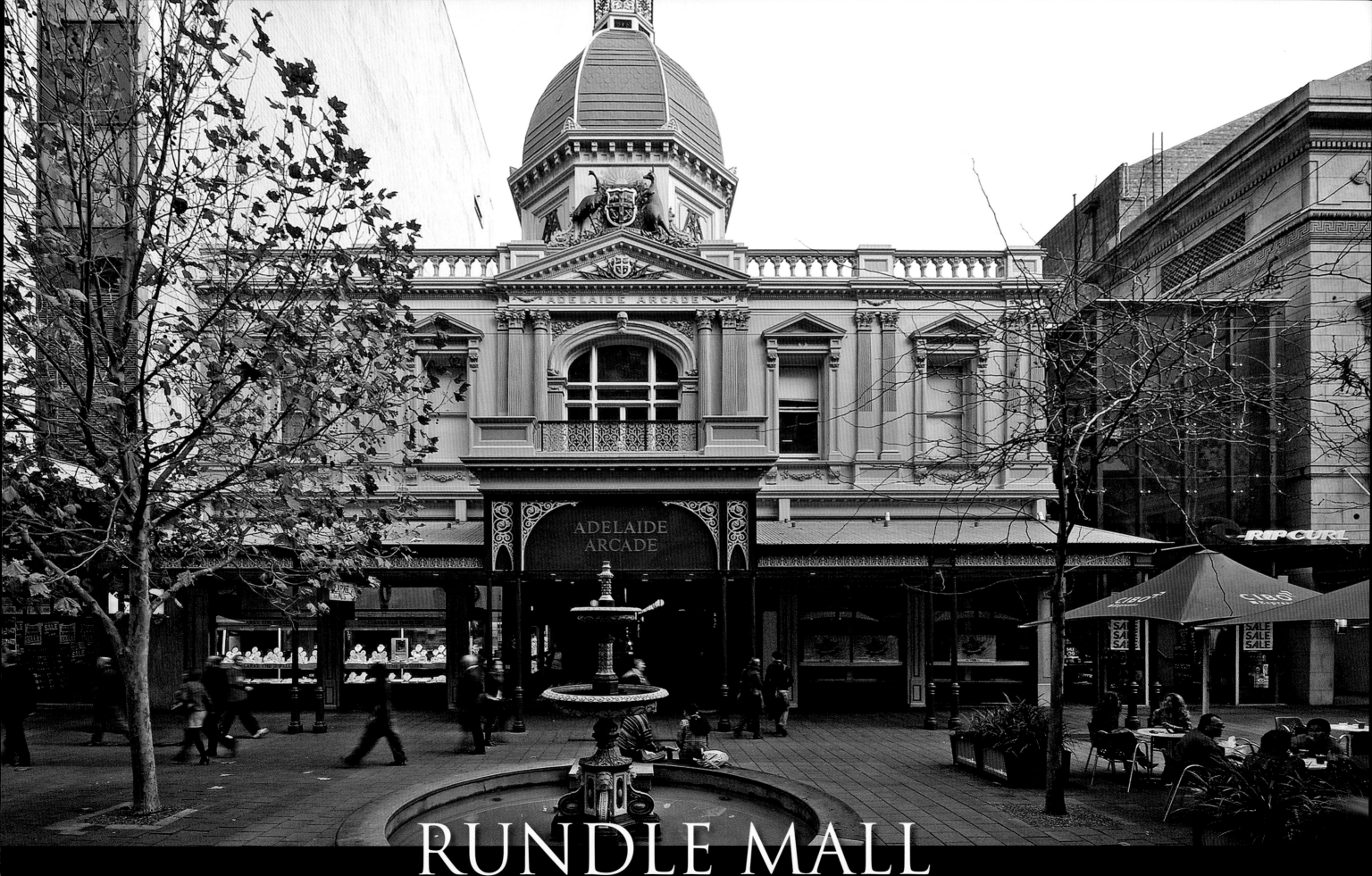

RUNDLE MALL

BEEHIVE BUILDING

KALAMAZOO (AUST.) LTD., 32 King William Street, Adelaide. Office Equipment. Cent. 6484. **HAIGH'S**, Chocolates and Confectionery. Best quality always. **SEWELL'S**, Florist, etc. **GEORGE ADAMS PTY. LTD.**, Cake Shop also 12 branches in Adelaide and suburbs. **SHOEGOODS**, No. 4 Store, 6 Rundle Street. Ladies' Shoe Specialists.

GEO. O. BROOK, E.S.M.G., Optometrist. C: 4135 **HOLSTEN'S**, Adelaide's leading milliners. **KATHLYN HECKER**, Leading Coat & Frock Specialist. 12 Rundle Street. Phone: C 4644 **GLASSONS** is Adelaide's Biggest Fashion Shop and Ladies' wear specialists. Glassons' stocks of silks, hoisery, gloves, neckwear, hand-bags, millinery, coats, costumes, frocks and furs are kept up to the minute in style and marked at prices you want to pay. Your visit of inspection is cordially invited. 16 & 18 Rundle Street. Phone: Central 5070.

BEEHIVE BUILDING (1895–1896)   6a TO 8 RUNDLE STREET (1880)   HOLSTEN'S   HECKER'S (1868)

KING WILLIAM STREET

RUNDLE MALL (NORTH SIDE), BETWEEN KING WILLIAM STREET AND STEPHENS PLACE

In the centenary and for years afterwards, this part of Rundle Mall could have been transported brick by brick from Charles Dickens's London. Of what's left from then, Holsten's has closed its eye to its original appearance; Hecker's has kept its open. Or is the building, still celebrating its survival, winking at us? Between it and Beehive Corner, 6a to 8 summarises the character of the 19th century Rundle Street.

In every field of endeavor—there is always one who takes the lead. Forging ahead to new high standards of quality and service the **MYER EMPORIUM** offers the finest products backed with the greatest resources available. "Manufactured by Myer's" means merchandise made of the finest raw materials by men—and women famed for their ability! "Distributed and sold by Myer's" means merchandise that is the finest possible value for money and every style trend correctly interpreted to help maintain Myer Fashion leadership. From the initial opening of its doors to Adelaide in October, 1928, the Myer Emporium commenced with an ideal, which briefly stated, aims at "Building a business that will never know completion; developing stocks and service to the needs of a growing clientele; winning confidence by verifying it, and striving ever to secure the satisfaction of every customer."

We rededicate this ideal in this proud year of South Australia's Centenary.

RUNDLE MALL (NORTH SIDE), BETWEEN KING WILLIAM STREET AND STEPHENS PLACE

MYER

What many of us remember as the "old" Myer Emporium had opened only eight years before *Progressive Adelaide* appeared. In the energised advertising prose of the day, Myer's offered "in this Centennial year a new conception of value in this Store – our 'Esprit de Corps' – new service!" The building that succeeded the emporium went one better. Dazzleland was an amusement park inside the billion dollar Myer Centre. It had a rollercoaster, dodgem cars and a hurdy gurdy, but the playground in the air didn't last.

STEPHENS PLACE

RUNDLE MALL (NORTH SIDE), BETWEEN STEPHENS PLACE AND GAWLER PLACE

RUNDLE MALL PLAZA, FORMER DAVID JONES
(1961–1963)

Charles Birks became David Jones in the early 1960s. David Jones later moved down to John Martin's, so this David Jones became Rundle Mall Plaza. Birks's original Victorian-style commercial emporium had maximum windows and minimum internal walls to make the most of natural light. In the revamp of the old David Jones, windows were added to do likewise and some of the classic Angaston marble was lost. The light streams in, yet a modern Adelaide landmark building becomes less minimalist, more complicated. Shoppers had to face life head-on in 1936. The Charles Birks department store spoke here of "severe drought" and "unprecedented economic disruptions". There was no TV then and radio was still in the breakfast show of its years, so Baring's print advertisements set the agenda. The centenary forced Charles Birks to celebrate an anniversary it may not have deemed necessary. The firm did not shirk the challenge.

H. RUCH'S on the second floor. Permanent Waving, Marcel, Water-Waving, Tinting, Trimming, and Hair Treatment, etc. Phone: C. 5913. **"ETHELLA"** (Mrs. E.L. Griffin), Dressmaker and Costumier, is at No. 307 on the third floor. Estimates given. **C.W. FRIEBE**, 316 Third Floor. Manufacturer's Agent. Dent's Gloves, Aertex Underwear, "Doctor" Flannels.

At No. 306a on the third floor is **MRS. MICHAEL AULD** Modiste, Dressmaking, and Alterations. **MISS D. WIESMEYER**, Dressmaker & Costumier, is situated at 315 on the third floor. Alterations a specialty. **MISS ELSIE GRAY'S** Ladies' Toilet Salon is on the fourth floor, No. 403. All branches of Hair Work. Tinting, Face and Scalp Massage, Manicuring etc. Permanent Waving a specialty. Phone: C. 1242. **F.L. RUNGE**, Fifth Floor,

Wholesale Representative "Paramount" E.P. and Brassware, Tennent's Clocks, "Down-ee" Traps, Premier Kitchenware, Marshall's Brass Screens, "Onoto" Pens, etc. **MISS TRAVERS**, 509a on the fifth floor. Costumier & Dressmaker. Phone: C. 8988. **W. PARK LOW** (late 28 years with Wendt's), fifth floor. Watches and clocks of all descriptions carefully repaired. **G. NANCARROW AND A. ROYANS**, Tailors and Costumiers, are situated on

the fifth floor. Latest fashions, combined with high-class workmanship, make our suits supreme. Phone: C. 3295. **L.A. GAINER** (late of Harris, Scarfe Ltd.), 609 Sixth floor. Specialist in repairs to all makes of watches and grandfather clocks. Workmanship guaranteed. Phone: C. 1575. **WILLIAM COWARD**, Engraver, Die-Sinker, Badge-Maker, etc., 610 Sixth Floor. Established 1900. Phone: 5968. Under Vice-Regal Patronage. **WHOLESALE**

FURRIERS LTD., 615 Sixth Floor. **GRACE BROS.**, Sixth Floor, Manufacturers' Representatives in Hardware, Fancy Goods, Upholsterers' Lines, etc. From the same office, **F.R. GRACE** conducts his business as a roof specialist, and **A.R. GRACE** his dental goods agencies. Phone: C. 1575. **R.W. DORLING**, Room 708, Seventh Floor. Trophy Engravers. Inscriptions to Cups, etc., Monograms, Crests. Armorial Bearings to Watches,

Signet Rings. Phone: C. 2375. **EVELYN TOY**, Milliner, is on the seventh floor. **MANUFACTURING FURRIERS**, Skin Pressers, Fur Dyers. Renovations a specialty. Phone: C. 2630.

WAXMAN'S, the outstanding Mantle specialists, are now showing their advanced display of New Season's Coats, Frocks, and Millinery at their Model Showroom, 76 Rundle Street.

JOHN MARTIN'S   A 100% South Australian Institution

● Founded in the year 1866 on Wednesday, October 24th, by Messrs. Peters and Martin, John Martin & Co., Limited has grown up at the same address since its inception and has remained entirely South Australian. Its growth and prosperity have always marched hand-in-hand with prosperity and growth of the State: On the firm's payroll to-day are more than 1,200 South Australians. . . . This Centenary Year marks the 70th birthday of John Martin's and it is fitting that visitors to Adelaide will see in the recently completed New Store an imposing structure as modern as any in Australasia. . . . It will be pointed out with pride to our visitors as a unique example of true progress. . . . A South Australian achievement by South Australians for South Australia.

YORK THEATRE

RUNDLE MALL (NORTH SIDE), BETWEEN GAWLER PLACE AND CHARLES STREET

EDMENTS BUILDING (1926)

FORMER BALFOURS CAFE (1924)

DAVID JONES

At top left, the York Theatre and York Chambers building, not so much a bookend but a slim volume on a corner, simply disappeared to allow a wider Gawler Place. Still standing is the time-honoured Edments Building. In Baring's day, among many tenants it housed Ruby Pugsley and Co., milliners under Vice-Regal patronage. Lady Dugan could take a short stroll from Government House to try on the very latest in hats. The Balfours Shop is heritage in every way, a cultural institution and a building to treasure. Its large window allows light to all floors, where for decades South Australians made shopping a day out by dining out. The centenary coincided with the 70th birthday of another South Australian institution, John Martin's, which was celebrated with a new store "as modern as any in Australia". Try as heritage conscious people did, they couldn't save the "Johnnies" building 60 years later. The David Jones, or "DJs", store in its place is a low maintenance modern commercial building.

One of Australia's most modern toilet salons is the **"CONTINENTAL" LADIES' TOILET SALON**, which is situated on the corner of Rundle and Charles Street. The entrance to this modern salon, which is downstairs, is at 36 Charles Street (opposite John Martin's). The Proprietors, Messrs. H. Anton and W. Walla are High-Class Ladies' Hairdressers. Phone: C. 2288.

SHOEGOODS, No. 2 Store, 110 Rundle Street. Ladies' Shoe Specialists. (Next door to Coles'.)

COLES STORES, Nothing over 2'6 Hosiery, Drapery, Boy's Wear, Men's Wear, Habardashery, Stationery, Confectionery, Hardware, Crockery, Glassware, Jewellery, Fancy Goods, Toilets and Hair Goods. Visit our quick service cafe. 112–118 Rundle Street.

METTERS LIMITED, 124 Rundle St. Branches and Works in Melbourne, Sydney, Perth, Brisbane, and Wellington, N.Z. The name of **METTERS** in conjunction with stoves and ranges; pumps and windmills, cast iron porcelain enamelware, hollowware, etc., is a household word throughout the whole of Australia. Phone: C. 6300.

Bridge Parties are a special feature of the **GREEN GATE CAFE**, Party Specialists, Richmond Arcade, Rundle Street. Light luncheons, morning and afternoon teas. All cakes are made on the premises.

RUNDLE MALL (NORTH SIDE), BETWEEN CHARLES STREET AND PULTENEY STREET

Above The Reject Shop sign, the ex-Coles department store is a surprise packet – a modernist terracotta building dating from 1940 that fits the Mall better than most. Further down the street, Metters made stoves, pumps and, as you can see, windmills for the man on the land and the suburban block. They were sold from an attractive classical concrete building, reminiscent of the ornate Freemasons Hall on North Terrace. Although its retail use couldn't be more different, the Metters building still works. After starting as the Cornwall then the Plough and Harrow, the Hotel Richmond has a licence only three years younger than South Australia. It has been rated one of Australia's top small hotels, and has art and ambience. From the little kikki.K stationery and gifts store, Gerard & Goodman once sold its Clipsal electrical supplies. Clipsal equals V8 racing cars in the Parklands, or "The Clipsal", SA's gift to the global sport.

FORMER COLES BUILDING
(1940)

FORMER METTERS BUILDING
(1902)

HOTEL RICHMOND
(1928)

KIKKI.K

KUHNEL & CO. LTD.

INTERIOR VIEW OF MANCHESTER HOUSE

THE HOME OF THE GLORY BOX CLUB
142 RUNDLE STREET – – ADELAIDE

NEXT DOOR TO THE NATIONAL BANK

MANCHESTER SPECIALISTS
DIRECT IMPORTERS

SAMUEL SMITH'S BUILDING (1887)

THE LEWIS   UNEMPLOYED
SHOE CO.   SALES DEPOT

MADAME TERESE, 140 Rundle Street, downstairs. Large range of Fancy Costumes Wedding Veils, etc., on hire. Phone: C. 1118.

MANCHESTER HOUSE The Home of **THE GLORY BOX CLUB**. 142 Rundle Street. Manchester specialists, direct importers.

GOLDRING'S, 150 Rundle Street, Millinery Specialists, are now showing a full range of New Season's Modes. ALL MODERATELY PRICED. Orders supplied promptly from our own work-rooms.

THE LEWIS SHOE CO. 152 Rundle Street. All classes of footware at lowest city prices. Huge selection. Established 25 years. Phone: C 5998

GOLDRING'S MILLINERY ASSURES SATISFACTION. Phone: C. 1892.

MISSES HASSE, DISTINCTIVE MILLINERY and Mantle Specialists, 156 Rundle Street, Adelaide.

RUNDLE MALL (NORTH SIDE), BETWEEN CHARLES STREET AND PULTENEY STREET

Kuhnel's Pianos and Organs building on the left is a loss, but next door is a fine 1920s commercial building that gives substance to the quieter end of Rundle Mall. The Depression still bit in the centenary year, as shown by the Unemployed Sales Depot in Samuel Smith's offices and shops building. Before Adelaide's take on skyscrapers, this place stood out in the retail district. In those early days it was not height, but detail, that caught the eye. This one has ornamentation in gold spades from The Lewis Shoe Co. all the way to the top.

ELLIOTT BROS. LTD., 147 Rundle St., of Super Elliott Cycle fame. Phone: C. 236.

DANKEL & CO., 145A Rundle St., Electrical Engineers and Suppliers. Radio and Refrigeration Specialists. Phone: C. 3648. (2 Lines).

MARTIN BUILDINGS

SILKS LIMITED, 143 Rundle Street, Silk Specialist, "The Ladies' Paradise." Silk Piece Goods of every description. **MAUDE F. PROSSER** 141 Rundle Street, Arts & Craft Studio. Designs for carving, metal work, leatherwork, and needlework. Furnishing a speciality. Classes for tapestry and other crafts. Phone: C. 4645. **CREEPER PHYSICAL CULTURE STUDIO**, 141 Rundle Street, Health and Strength Specialist. Phone: C. 4033. **ELSIE V. HOOPER**, moderate price dressmaker, 9 and 10 first floor, (end of corridor). Workroom under Mrs. Holman's management. Phone: C. 7320. **DOROTHY HOOPER** (late Lyons and Hooper), on the same floor. Dressmaker and Costumier. **TROUSSEAU LTD.**, specialises in Ladies' Underwear, Hosiery, and Aprons.

INTERIOR VIEW OF PORTION OF SHOWROOMS
OF
SILKS LIMITED
143 RUNDLE STREET

Reproduction of work of

MAUDE F. PROSSER,

Martin Buildings, 141 Rundle Street, Adelaide.

MAUDE F. PROSSER

ARTS & CRAFT STUDIO

MARTIN BUILDINGS

141 RUNDLE STREET, ADELAIDE

DESIGNS FOR CARVING, METAL WORK, LEATHERWORK, AND NEEDLEWORK

FURNISHING A SPECIALITY

CLASSES FOR TAPESTRY AND OTHER CRAFTS

'Phone: C. 4645

PULTENEY STREET

RUNDLE MALL (SOUTH SIDE), BETWEEN PULTENEY STREET AND TWIN STREET

Rundle Street became Rundle Mall in September 1976, by decree of Premier Dunstan. The former Clarkson's building was where South Australia went for its glazing requirements. Built as a butcher's shop, the place had the first commercial electric lighting, switched on in 1882. The City Council has a permanent rolling master plan to keep and build on the Mall's appeal. One challenge is the modernised ground level shopfronts; rarely do they distinguish one building from the next. You have to look higher for that, to where the Council is hoping to encourage renewed commercial and residential activity in many long neglected spaces.

FORMER CLARKSON'S BUILDING (1880)

DELL'S BUILDING (1927)

TWIN STREET

RUNDLE MALL (SOUTH SIDE), BETWEEN TWIN STREET AND ADELAIDE ARCADE

BIBLE HOUSE

ADELAIDE ARCADE (1885)

Nobody should put a building on a long, narrow site unless they have a good idea for it. Dell's Building, now Bible House, was a good idea. With its corner site, the Federation classical-style building still has the mettle to make people stop and enjoy. Pity about the external air conditioners. Like the Festival Theatre before the Sydney Opera House, Adelaide Arcade beat Sydney's Strand Arcade and Melbourne's Block Arcade as the very latest in sophisticated 19th century shopping precincts. Soon after, the adjoining Gay's Arcade became Adelaide Arcade's sunroom. Originally, upstairs was workspace, then it became shops. With its sister ship the Exhibition Building on North Terrace sadly long gone, Adelaide Arcade alone is history and charm at shopping pace. Attracting human traffic along the upper level remains a mission.

ADELAIDE ARCADE

THE PALACE BILLIARD HALLS, above the Arcade, supply the trade, and are the only direct importers of Billiards Requisites in South Australia.

BRONSON'S, First Shop from Rundle Street. Dyers, Dry Cleaners, and Repairing Tailors. Phone C. 4408.

"VIGNOLA" COFFEE LOUNGE, 6, 8, and 10 New Modern Arcade. Morning teas, afternoon teas, late suppers in a Comfortable and Refined atmosphere. Open till 2 a.m.

E. BOWEN, No. 12, Jeweller and Diamond Ring Maker. Repairs a Speciality.

At No. 14 in the Arcade is the General Engraving Business of **H.E. LUCY**, who does all Brass Plates and Embossed Number Plates. Phone C. 6674.

CATHOLIC REPOSITORY (J.P. Hansen), 16 Arcade. Devotional Requisites. Altar Supplies, Catholic, and General Literature.

Ladies are advised that the **YASMIN TOILET SALON**, Waving Specialists, is at No. 32. Phone C. 2980.

P.T. SPICER, Ladies and Gentlemen's Tailor, is at No. 40 in this Arcade. Phone C. 5980.

BUTLER'S (Richard Butler & Sons), No. 46, Adelaide's Leading Umbrella, Sunshade, Walking Stick, and Cutlery Specialists. Forty-five years' practical experience. The proprietors of Adelaide Doll's Hospital.

ADELAIDE ARCADE (LOOKING SOUTH)

ADELAIDE ARCADE (LOOKING NORTH)

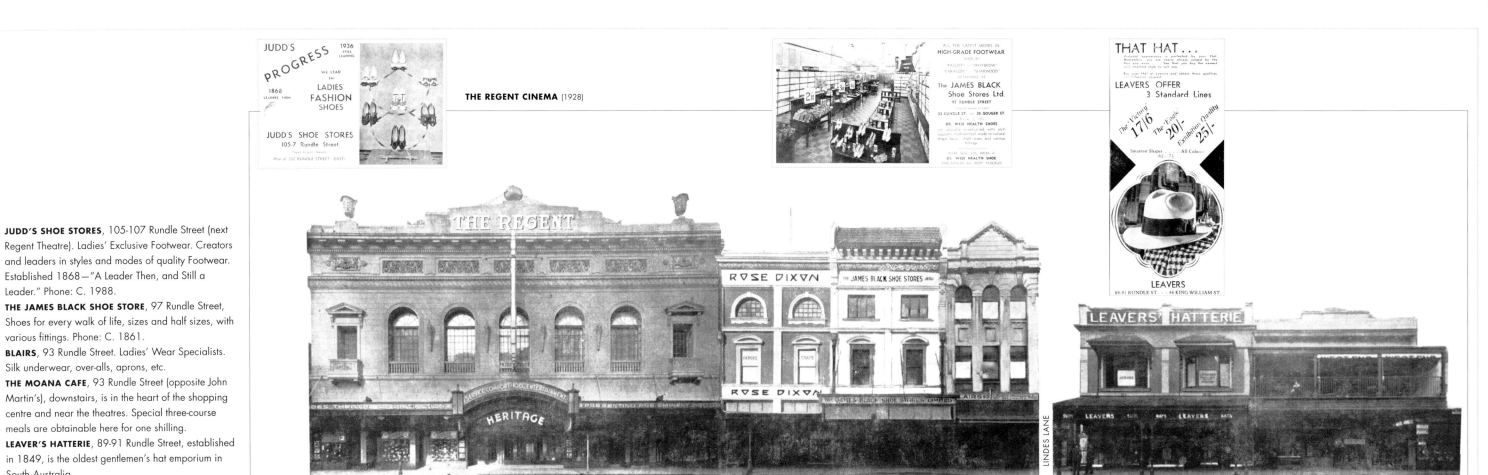

JUDD'S SHOE STORES, 105-107 Rundle Street (next Regent Theatre). Ladies' Exclusive Footwear. Creators and leaders in styles and modes of quality Footwear. Established 1868—"A Leader Then, and Still a Leader." Phone: C. 1988.

THE JAMES BLACK SHOE STORE, 97 Rundle Street, Shoes for every walk of life, sizes and half sizes, with various fittings. Phone: C. 1861.

BLAIRS, 93 Rundle Street. Ladies' Wear Specialists. Silk underwear, over-alls, aprons, etc.

THE MOANA CAFE, 93 Rundle Street (opposite John Martin's), downstairs, is in the heart of the shopping centre and near the theatres. Special three-course meals are obtainable here for one shilling.

LEAVER'S HATTERIE, 89-91 Rundle Street, established in 1849, is the oldest gentlemen's hat emporium in South Australia.

THE REGENT CINEMA (1928)

RUNDLE MALL (SOUTH SIDE), BETWEEN REGENT ARCADE AND HARRIS SCARFE

When Baring clicked, the Regent was showing Charles Chauvel's *Heritage*, about the emergence of modern Australia – its heritage. That's an irony, because the glamorous picture palace at the heart of South Australia's cinema-going heritage is now no more than a facade. The Regent coincided with the arrival of the talkies. Musicians who had made a good living playing for the silents found themselves out on the streets, so they performed there. "Dirty Dick" and his tin whistle did not always endear, while "Piccolo Pete" drove the Regent's manager almost to distraction. Today's busking is, like Bert Flugelman's Mall's Balls and the brass pigs, part of Rundle Mall life, usually much appreciated.

REGENT ARCADE   MALL'S BALLS
                       (1977)

WALSH'S ORIENTAL

Adelaide's Oldest and Most Popular Residential Hotel

Cable and Telegraph: "Oriental" 'Phone: C. 1130

Interior Views of the Oriental.

LOUNGE

ONE OF THE SALOON BARS

SMOKE LOUNGE

DINING ROOM

DOUBLE BEDROOM

SINGLE BEDROOM

The Oriental stands on a site—the south-eastern corner of Rundle Street and Gawler Place—in the centre of the business and amusement houses.

In 1848, 12 years after the foundation of the colony, a Public House was erected and named the Hamburg Hotel, which name was retained until 1915, when the present owner, Mr. H. R. Walsh, purchased the property, and renamed it "The Oriental".

At present a modern five storey building carries on the traditions of goodwill that have been handed down through 88 years of Progress.

The Oriental has recently been remodelled, and every facility for comfort and convenience has been incorporated in the Hotel, with 50 exclusive bedrooms, each containing such innovations as hot and cold water, telephones, reading lamps, and writing desks.

Bedrooms de Luxe with Bathroom, etc. are also available.

The Cuisine is of an extremely high standard, and is dispensed by a staff well-known throughout Australia for efficiency and service.

Private Dining Rooms are available for Dinners, Weddings, Bridge Parties, etc.

Reduced inclusive tariff from 17/6 per day.

Under the management and personal supervision of the proprietors, Mr. and Mrs. Herbert R. Walsh.

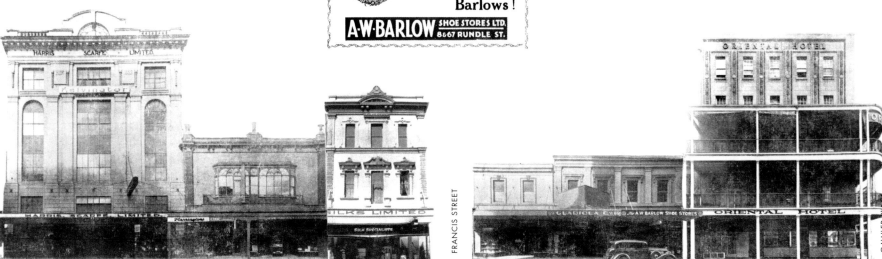

FRANCIS STREET

GAWLER PLACE

RUNDLE MALL (SOUTH SIDE), BETWEEN HARRIS SCARFE AND GAWLER PLACE

HARRIS SCARFE BUILDING
(demolished 2011)

WALSH BUILDING (1925, 1937)

Mick Bradley photographed the most important surviving commercial store building in Rundle Mall just before it disappeared. The 1920s Palazzo-style Harris Scarfe had original cast iron pillars, pressed metal decorative ceilings and a place in the South Australian vernacular. It is making way for a 19-storey tower called Rundle Place. At the opposite end, Walsh's Oriental Hotel, now just the Walsh Building, is largely untouched on the outside and a going concern on the inside. The heritage people would like to see more of similar around the city's streets.

BIRKS CHEMISTS LIMITED, are now the owners of Pharmacy Building, 57 Rundle St., and the business which was started by George Napier and William Hanson Birks in the year 1856. Phone: C. 1414.

BLACK'S LIMITED

R.V. THOMAS SPORTS GOODS, 53 Rundle Street, specialising in sporting Goods and Repairs, both Wholesale and Retail. A big staff of experts ensures quality goods from all the leading manufacturers. Phone: C. 2957.

ALLANS MUSIC

CHAS. WALTER & SONS 45 Rundle St. are the oldest established tailoring specialists in Adelaide. Phone: C. 653.

MARGARET DAVOREN ROBE SPECIALISTS. New season's Millinery, Blouses, Robes, Coats, and Evening Wear at 45a. Phone: C. 6039.

STENNET'S BEAUTY SALON is at 45b. Phone: C. 5191.

WAXMAN'S, Mantle Specialists, of 43 Rundle St, for distinction in Coats, Frocks, and Millinery. "A thing of beauty is a joy for ever." Be satisfied at **LAUREL TOILET SALON** 43 Rundle St. Phone: C. 4446.

CENTRAL PROVISION STORES, 41 Rundle St, High-Class Grocers, Provision, and Tea Merchants. Phone: C. 1263.

F. RANDLE, Costume, Coat, and Frock Specialist, third floor. Phone: C. 6990.

MISS HELEY, Dressmaker and Costumier. second floor. Phone: C.8971.

MARIE SMITH'S TOILET SALON, 39 Rundle St., above **ROGERS**. Permanent Wave Specialists. Phone: C. 6973.

THE CHARMIAN TOILET SALON is situated upstairs at 31 Rundle St. All branches of Ladies' Hairdressing are executed here by skilled assistants, under personal supervision. For appointments phone: C. 8697.

SAVERY'S PIANOS LIMITED, 29 Rundle St. S.A. Distributors: L Beale, Weissbrod Pianos; Stromberg-Carlson and Cremona Radio; Kelvinator Domestic Refrigeration; A.B.C. Washers; Hamilton Beach Vacuum Cleaners; Savery's Sewing Machines; Savery's Broadcasting Service (5DN). Phone: C. 8000.

RUNDLE MALL (SOUTH SIDE), BETWEEN GAWLER PLACE AND JAMES PLACE

BIRKS BUILDING (1925)

FORMER ALLANS BUILDING (1870, 1925)

Birks on the corner and Black's next to it have survived with different identities – both good-looking, confident buildings. Upstairs behind the glazed bricks of the latter, still branded with its original C.J. Young Shoe Co., the velvet drapes and wooden shoe shelving remain. Those were the days when a shop assistant X-rayed your feet for the perfect fit. Allans Music next door, the building with the nose job today, later moved around the corner to Gawler Place. But in the State's centenary year it marked the eastern entrance to Adelaide's music enclave. Further along, Savery's Pianos also sold washing machines. Immediately west of the old Allans, a couple of the street's livelier buildings are much plainer in the Mall now. They could be a case for giving the Adelaide Festival's Northern Lights projections a commercial application.

S. SIGALAS & CO. (L. Vidale, Proprietor), 19 Rundle St. Wholesale & Retail Confectionery & Chocolate Manufacturers. Specialists in the preparation of Ice Creams and Milk drinks, hot or cold. Established over 30 years. Phone: C. 1874.

The firm of **CAWTHORNES LTD.**, est.1870 is the oldest-established music and musical instrument house in the Southern Hemisphere. Good service and quality goods are the staple lines on which this business has been founded.17a Rundle St. Phone: C. 1328.

HELMER'S Adelaide's Leading specialists in Frocks, Coats, Millinery. Ladies! Be well dressed in a Helmer gown. 17 & 66 Rundle St. Phone: C. 3731

RED LION HOTEL, Eddie McCarron, Prop. Est. over 90 years. Phone: C. 1213.

JEAN ANDRE, 13 Rundle St. Ladies' Handbag Salon. Devoted to supplying the handbag needs of Adelaide's womenfolk.

HOLSTENS, Adelaide's Leading Millinery Specialists, of 11 Rundle St. Holsten's show the very latest fashions from London, Paris, and New York. They have their own large workrooms.

Hats and hand-made gifts can be obtained from **MISS V. SIDOLI**, 9 Rundle St. Children's Hats a speciality. C. 3147.

SANITARIUM HEALTH FOOD SHOP AND VEGETARIAN CAFE, 7a Rundle St. Nut and dried fruit specialists. Manufacturers of Wholemeal Bread, cakes, etc. Phone: C. 1826.

G.W. COX, 3 Rundle Street, up-to-date Watchmakers, Jewellers, and Gold Buyers. Established 40 years.

Alfred Drake's
MAYFAIR THEATRE (1916)

JAMES PLACE

KING WILLIAM STREET

RUNDLE MALL (SOUTH SIDE), BETWEEN JAMES PLACE AND KING WILLIAM STREET

Alfred Drake wasn't afraid to let the world know what he was up to. "ERECTED BY ALFRED DRAKE 1916" is all that remains below where "Grand" and "Mayfair" once indicated his ambitious picture theatre. A publican until his showbiz moment, proud Alf reasoned that showing Chaplin, Keaton, Fairbanks and Pickford directly opposite the Myer Emporium would be good for the box office. He was right, after a fashion, until 1976 when the Lotteries moved in. The twee building next door would bring a sentimental tear even to the eye of the departed. Sigalas, "Specialists in the preparation of Ice Creams and Milk Drinks", in the 1936 photo had been there 30 years, and had another 50 to go. For generations it was where a boy took a girl for a milk shake and first love. Sigalas was cool before the word was used that way. It's gone now but the name still means the same to everyone who shared a straw there. Next door again, Cawthornes was the oldest music business in the southern hemisphere until it moved a few doors east and became Savery-Cawthorne Music World. Scott's Menswear took its place, and every baby boomer teenager worth his tartan-cuffed bell bottoms dressed out of there.

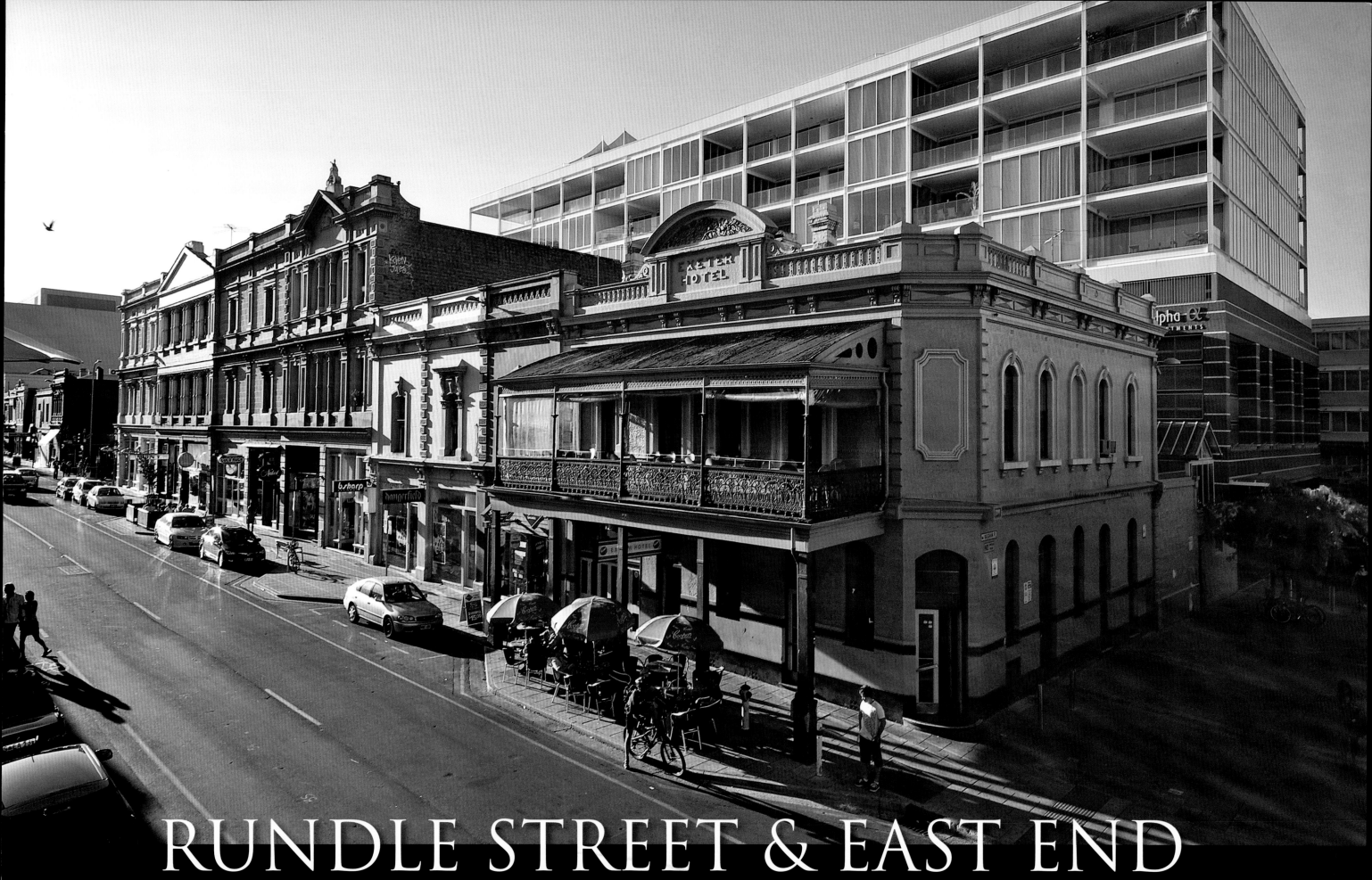

RUNDLE STREET & EAST END

METRO SYMPHONY FURNISHERS, Office and Showrooms, 180 Rundle Street (opposite Foy's) are Specialists in Furniture, Radio, Refrigerators, Records, Pianos, and Electrical Goods. South Australian Representatives for Symphony and Weldon Radio and Distributors of Airzone, Radiola, and Astor. Phone: C. 1656.

RUNDLE BUILDINGS

CORAL LEE, 182 Rundle Street, Frock Specialist, showing Sydney's latest styles. Smartest and most exclusive fashions at unbeatable prices are always obtainable at this store.

SANDERS' RUBBER STORE, 186 Rundle Street. "The Rubber Specialists." Sanders' huge stock comprise everything in rubber. All classes of Rubber Goods repaired. Phone: C. 2488.

H. GRUNDY & CO., Boot Manufacturers, 186-188 Rundle Street (opposite Foy & Gibson's). "From factory to foot." Oldest established makers of every description of boots and shoes in Adelaide. Grundy's have been faithfully supplying the public of South Australia for over 50 years. Phone: C. 1988.

CRAVENS

PULTENEY STREET

SYNAGOGUE PLACE

RUNDLE STREET (NORTH SIDE), BETWEEN PULTENEY STREET AND SYNAGOGUE PLACE

RUNDLE BUILDINGS
(1896, facade 1936)

Before shopping centres and shopping towns, Adelaide families caught the tram, train or bus into what everyone called "town". Department stores like Cravens flourished. Big store turned into bigger car park seemed to be a fate pre-ordained at this end of Rundle Street. There are some great survivors, just the same. Grundy's on the corner has been selling boots and shoes in the same spot for more than 120 years. "From factory to foot", says the advertising in 1936. Owners the Whittenbury family have been in the store for almost 90 years. Great location, no reason to move, explains manager Damien Whittenbury. A recent Grundy's renovation retained the historic exterior mosaic tiles and added some old-time light boxes. The firm's home, Rundle Buildings, is linked to the church around the corner, the Synagogue, the place of worship for Adelaide's Jewish community since its first construction in 1850. The Synagogue and Rundle Buildings were refronted to look like the picture theatres in the 1930s. South Australia was founded on religious tolerance, so a little freedom with church architecture didn't go astray.

GARNAUT'S SHOE STORE, at 196, has all the latest in Boots and Shoes. Repairs a speciality. **GARNAUT'S NEWSAGENCY AND STATIONERY STORE** is at 196a Rundle Street. Latest periodicals.

"THE OLD CURIOSITY SHOP" (Miss V.H. Wood), 200 Rundle Street. High-Class China, Antiques, Glass, Antique Furniture. Good bought and sold. Phone: C. 6322.

SUPREME FURNISHERS
MODERN AND ARTISTIC FURNITURE AND FURNISHINGS
206 RUNDLE STREET EAST (Next Rundle Street P.O.)

PENGELLY & KNABE, Undertakers and Cremators—established 1865—are at 210 Rundle Street. This is one of the oldest-established undertaking firms in the State. Phone: C. 496.

GEO. CLARK, 212 Rundle St, Diploma of Fellowship British Horological Institute, London, 1917. Practical Watch and Clock-Maker. Highest awards Adelaide Jubilee Exhibition, 1887, 1891, 1895, 1900, 1905.

SYNAGOGUE PLACE

FROME STREET

RUNDLE STREET (NORTH SIDE), BETWEEN SYNAGOGUE PLACE AND FROME STREET

SYNAGOGUE

SUPER ELLIOTTS (1938) **FORMER RUNDLE STREET POST OFFICE** (1938)

Super Elliotts started out selling bicycles in Rundle Street in 1902 and had its own crack racing team. It was on the verge of establishing its present store in a cycling boom when Baring passed by. Today bikes are back and the Tour Down Under often starts nearby. After 99 years undertakers Pengelly & Knabe left Rundle Street for Greenhill Road and an eventual name change to Blackwell Funerals. Parking had become a problem and the chapel was too small, although coffins were still made upstairs where the Knabe family once lived. On the weekend of the big shift the firm's first 45 years of records, in leather-bound books, were accidentally consigned to the tip. For a team of morticians that was a grievous loss, as it was to South Australian history.

TAVISTOCK HOTEL

BOWDEN'S Smart Shoe Repair Service is at 230. Repairs are executed here while you wait.

GEO. LANDERS, Saddler and Harness-Maker, is also at 230. Racing and Trotting Gear.

THE WILLOW CAFE (C. Stathis Proprietor) 234 Rundle Street. High-Class 3 course meals. Reasonable price.

MOTOR SUPPLIES, 236 Rundle Street. Everything for the motor. Batteries, Tyres, Accessories, Spares, Retreading. Service by certified mechanics. Best prices. Technical advice free. Phone: C. 549. **COLIN RODGER,** Jeweller and Watchmaker, is at No. 236. Repairs a speciality. Phone: C. 549.

At 240 is **BRAMMY & CO.,** Boot-Makers and Shoe Repairers. Expert workmanship.

No. 242a is the Refreshment Rooms of **W.A. AND E. STRUTHERS.** Grills and Luncheons are obtainable at all hours. Centenary visitors specially catered for.

At 244, next to the Exeter Hotel, is **BOB GIBBERD'S SHOE STORE.** Noted for heavy and medium Watertight Boots.

THE EXETER HOTEL (Bert Rook, Proprietor) is on the corner of Vaughan Place. First class accommodation. Reasonable Tariff. Best brands of wine and spirits. Also West End Ales on draught. Phone: L 4259.

TAVISTOCK BUILDINGS (1882–1885) **TAVISTOCK TERRACES** **FORMER STRUTHERS' REFRESHMENT ROOMS** **EXETER HOTEL**

The Tavistock Hotel was reduced to dust in the 1960s when the Council widened Tavistock Street to create Frome Street. The grand plan was to build a major road through to Wakefield Street, then maybe all the way to South Terrace and on to National Highway One. Traffic ruled the city. Sanity prevailed in half measure; the devastation of Rundle Street East went no further. The East End could breathe again. It always has had a mind of its own. It began as a village within the city square mile, home to the East End Market and later also the Adelaide Fruit and Produce Exchange. People now live above the shops that served the market workers. Starting with the western mural wall where the hotel once stood, the surviving Italianate sandstone Tavistock Terraces are keepsakes of a long ago prosperity. Two doors to the east of there were Struthers' Refreshment Rooms. "Centenary visitors specially catered for", said the Struthers. If they meant visitors to their shop, that could have meant the red carpet treatment for everybody in South Australia, all year. So business should have been brisk in 1936. On the corner, the front bar of the Exeter Hotel is shrine to departed Viking street adult and walking wardrobe Christos Juhanson – along with hundreds of other social and intellectual animals who choose to question the conventions of life. The Exeter balcony is where they graze and gaze.

H.S. CHAPMAN, Watchmaker, established 45 years, at No. 258, is official repairer to Commonwealth and S.A. Railways.

CHINA IMPORT CO., 260 Rundle St. Importers & wholesale distributors confectionery, fruit syrups, nuts, fresh fruit, paper, bags, tobacco cigarettes, fireworks, etc. Phone: C. 1591.

WRIGHT'S CYCLE WORKS, 262 Rundle Street, buys, sells and exchanges Radios and Cycles. Repairs.

JUDD'S SHOE STORES, 262a Rundle Street East. Established 1868. Suppliers of strong and reliable Boots and Shoes to the gardener and producer for over 65 years.

L. TIGHE & CO. LTD., 264 Rundle Street, have everything for the poultry-keeper and bird fancier. Phone: C. 4376.

T.P. WHITBREAD, 266 Rundle Street, General Saddler and Harness-Maker. All repairs done. Phone: C. 3419.

Three-course meals for one shilling are obtainable at **THE CANBERRA CAFE,** 268 Rundle Street. Quality, cleanliness, and quick service are special features.

S.O. BEILBY GROCER AND PROVISION MERCHANT, 270-272 Rundle Street, Adelaide. Central 5707.

VAUGHAN PLACE

RUNDLE STREET EAST (NORTH SIDE), BETWEEN VAUGHAN PLACE AND EAST END CINEMAS

FORMER S.O. BEILBY (1907)

S.O. Beilby was known as "Adelaide's quality cut-price grocer", "SA's greatest grocer" and a "high-class chain store grocer". The firm started by Sydney Beilby sold out to Coles in 1959. Here it traded out of the old Charlick's store. Adelaide was more tea than coffee in 1936, and Beilby's sold chests full. Today the aroma is coffee everywhere on the way to the cinemas around the corner.

EDWIN PARKS, Baker and Pastry-cook, 278 Rundle Street, has served generations satisfactorily for 52 years. Phone: C. 1988.

The evolution of the **"GREEN SHOP"** marks the result of 25 years of business experience of **MR. G.A. MOYSE** in the east of Rundle Street.

J.W. JOHNSTON, Tailor, Hatter, and Mercer, is at 284 Rundle Street East. Phone: C. 4343.

J.L. FREARSON, 288a Rundle Street, Hardware Showrooms. Paints, Fencing, Wire, Cement Irrigation Piping, etc.

At 298 is **MCDONALD'S FRUIT AND COOL DRINK SHOP**. Hall's Stone Ginger Beer and Pike's Tonic Ale are on draught here at threepence per handle. Phone: C. 464.

E.B. COX & CO., LTD., on the corner of East Terrace. Wholesale and Retail Seedsmen. All classes of Flower, Vegetable, Grass and Farm Seeds, Plants, Fruit Trees and Shrubs (in season). Also Foods and Medicines for all birds, animals, and fish, and Spray Mixtures for every purpose. Phone: C. 904.

CONRAD'S ENTRANCE

EAST TERRACE

RUNDLE STREET EAST (NORTH SIDE), BETWEEN EAST END CINEMAS AND EAST TERRACE

FORMER CONRAD'S BUTCHER SHOP (1905)

Mr Moyse at No. 280 was ahead of his environmental time with his Green Shop, "your assurance of successful Gardening". Where he hung his stag ferns is now a gelato parlour franchise, but the Green Movement, which is all about successful, sustainable gardening, continues to demand such assurances. At the former Johnston tailor's shop nearby, the verandah has been restored and a balcony added in one of city heritage's better outcomes. One along, the brilliant red brick and terracotta Edwardian building is now a nightclub and in better shape today. This time, it's a recycling outcome. Next door once more, the corner Conrad's Entrance was outside a thoroughfare to the East End Market. It took its name from the original Conrad's butcher's shop, the last to go from the East End. Leopold Conrad had two architect sons, Albert and Frank. Albert designed what became West's Coffee Palace at the other end of town for Leo. Frank refitted the butcher's shop, a popular restaurant these days. The tradition of a Stone Ginger Beer mentioned in the McDonald's advertisement above continued in the same spot for another 30 years. Nobody forgets a cold "Stonie".

**FORMER ADELAIDE FRUIT AND
PRODUCE EXCHANGE** (1903)

EAST TERRACE (WEST SIDE), BETWEEN GRENFELL STREET AND NORTH TERRACE

FORMER EAST END MARKET (1869)

The Adelaide Fruit and Produce Exchange is a bowl of Piccadilly strawberries and cream to the East End Market's bag of A1 Summertown spuds. The Exchange emerged at the time of the new nation called Australia, so its style is Federation with a Norton Summit cherry on top. This facade says it all. The hills and the river plains made Adelaide a garden. On either side of Rundle Street the Market and the Exchange distributed the garden's bounty around the city. The East End Market was Adelaide's first market on a large scale. For more than a century on market days, East Terrace was fruit 'n' veg on the move, followed by early breakfast or a beer. The movement only ceased a generation ago. Now this East Terrace is for coffee, the morning sun and the sweep across the road of Adelaide's Park Lands. Tucked away in the old Market space, the Palace and its nearby sister cinema the Nova are the only remaining picture theatres on a city strip that once glowed with them.

The freshest fruit and vegetables money could buy . . .

THE STAG HOTEL (Frank Choules, Proprietor), is on the corner of Rundle Street and East Terrace. Good accommodation. Moderate tariff. Beautiful view of gardens and hills from balconies. Phone: L 4626.

THE NEW MARKET RESIDENTIAL CAFE AND DINING ROOMS, 277 Rundle Street.

EAST TERRACE

VARDON AVENUE

RUNDLE STREET EAST (SOUTH SIDE), BETWEEN EAST TERRACE AND VARDON AVENUE

STAG HOTEL (1849, 1903)

The Stag Hotel, meeting place and watering hole for the eastern villagers bringing their produce to market, had a brief other life near the end of the 20th century. "They're coming into Stag Corner" went around the globe along with images of the pub's crowded balcony during the 11 years of the Australian Formula One Grand Prix. Some of the world's best racing drivers didn't make it around the testing second-gear bend. But the hotel with the octagonal corner turret and cast iron crown visible through the Park Lands trees is still going strong. In 1936, the New Market Residential Cafe and Dining Rooms in Market Chambers supplied "High-class Three Course Meals for one shilling". The building has remained true to form, joining others such as the next door Fruit and Produce Exchange entrance in a restaurant quarter that is at the forefront of alfresco dining in Adelaide.

EBENEZER PLACE

UNION STREET

RUNDLE STREET EAST (SOUTH SIDE), BETWEEN VARDON AVENUE AND UNION STREET

CHARLICK'S BUILDING (1927)

NOVA CINEMA

Mrs Reynolds's East End Ham Shop at No. 255 offered "Cold Luncheons, Ham and Eggs, Sandwiches, Smallgoods etc . . . obtainable here at all hours". From 1942, Ruby Jones took over, and fed the early morning market workers the same gear. No swearing or spitting allowed, or breakfast had to be left unfinished. Later Ruby's Cafe shone again at the other end of the day as a restaurant. The Maras Group, an active developer in the East End, now occupies the historic Charlick's Building, where blended tea, milled flour and bran and pollard once ruled the floorboards. *Progressive Adelaide* was about the commercial in 1936, not the residential. A large cottage with front garden stood on most of the ground where the Nova Cinema is. The cottage became a shooting gallery, but that wasn't business enough to save it from Baring's cutting room floor.

History of the State on Its Hundredth Birthday.

THE HISTORY OF FURNITURE.

The largest and most prominent Furniture Emporium in the State was founded at Broken Hill about the year 1885 by the late Mr. Malcolm Donald Reid.

A sub-divided shed being first utilised to display four completely furnished rooms, which were thrown open to Public inspection. So successful was this novel scheme of display that the firm made remarkable progress, and soon after was transferred to Franklin Street, Adelaide, where large premises were secured.

So phenomenal was the growth of the business that in 1909 the Company was able to purchase an important site in Rundle Street, Adelaide, where the large, imposing premises shown above are devoted exclusively to the display and sale of Furniture, Carpets, Linoleums, Furnishings, utilising approximately three acres of Floor space; the famous twenty-one Model Furnished rooms (which are the finest of their kind in the Southern Hemisphere), occupying the entire top floor of the building.

AN INVITATION

TO INSPECT THESE PALATIAL SHOWROOMS AND 21 MODEL ROOMS
IS CORDIALLY EXTENDED YOU

MALCOLM REID & CO. LTD.

Adelaide's Greatest and Most Spacious Furniture Emporium, 187-195 Rundle Street, East of Foy's.

THIS VIEW SHOWS THE MODERN AND WELL APPOINTED

MIXED LOUNGE
of

W. and Edith M. Garratt's

HOTEL AUSTRAL

205 RUNDLE STREET

(near Foy's)

ADELAIDE

YOU CAN HAVE YOUR LIQUID REFRESHMENT IN COMFORT AND BE ASSURED OF TRUE HOSPITALITY AT THE AUSTRAL

There is no room in "THE GREEN SHOP"

For Anything of Inferior Quality.

Remember This:
We Specialise in the BEST.

Seedlings
Shrubs
Trees
Cut Flowers

"The GREEN SHOP" selects from the Finest Nurseries in the State

"The Green Shop"

Graceful Ferns
and Palms
Rock Plants
Everything for the Garden

"The Green Shop" is your assurance of successful Gardening.

G. A. MOYSE, Sole Proprietor

280 Rundle St. East.

EXQUISITE GIFTS
FROM THE ORIENT

TREASURED GIFTS OF THE LOVELIEST
HANDWORKED TABLE LINENS
HANDKERCHIEFS — DAINTY LINGERIE
GORGEOUS KIMONOS AND SLIPPERS
SHINING BRASSWARE — CLOISONNE
MANDARIN CHINA
CARVED CAMPHORISED GLORY BOXES
As Well as Many Quaint Curios Which Add
Charm and Beauty to Every Home

陳公司 CHINA GIFT STORE
Miss SYM CHOON

"YOUR INSPECTION WILL BE APPRECIATED"

235-237 Rundle Street, East

CHINA GIFT STORE (Miss Sym Choon), 237 Rundle Street. Varieties of exquisite Chinese Hand-Worked Kimonas, Pyjamas, and Lingerie, etc.

SYM CHOON & CO., LTD., 233-235 Rundle Street. Nut Specialists and Merchants. P.O. Box X9. Phone: C. 4857.

COPP & CO., Rundle Street Booksellers, Stationers, and Newsagents. Half century of service to public.

NAN'S BEAUTY SHOP, 229 Rundle St. (Miss M. Humble). All classes of ladies' hairdressing. Phone: C. 3463.

TEMBY BROS., the up-to-date Tailors and Ladies' Costumiers, are at 227 Rundle Street. Suits hand-tailored.

The close proximity to the wholesale market of **THE I.X.L. FRUIT SHOP** is an assurance of the choicest Fruit and Vegetables. 225 Rundle Street.

F.F. CLEMENT, 223 Rundle St, Seedsman and Grain Merchant, established 1894. All Farm and Garden Seeds, Fertilizers, Fruit Trees, Roses, and Shrubs. Tomato Plants in season. Bird requisites. Country orders receive prompt attention.

GEO. CRAIG, 221 Rundle Street. The home of high-grade Bicycles. Craig Special and Sport Bicycles. Sundries and tyres of all descriptions supplied. Established 1894. Phone: C. 724.

FOGLIAS, Birds and Animals. Exporters and importers of Native and Foreign Birds and Animals. A wide range of rare and common fauna always on hand. 219 Rundle Street. Breeding station—Glenelg. Established 1880.

ERN BENNETTS, Ladies' and Gentlemen's Hairdresser and Tobacconist, is at 217 Rundle Street.

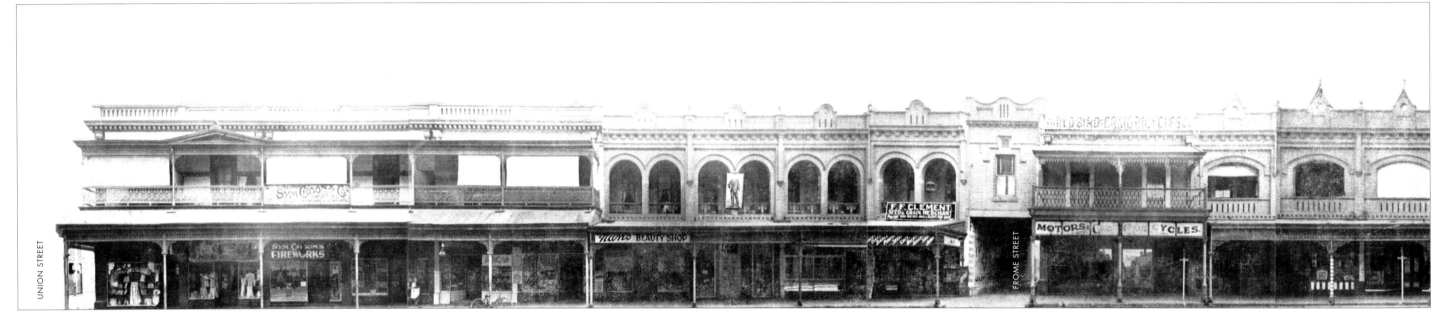

RUNDLE STREET EAST (SOUTH SIDE), BETWEEN UNION STREET AND FROME STREET

MISS GLADYS SYM CHOON

The stone terrace of six shops and residences that begins on the Union Street corner was built by the South Australian Company in 1898. Most famously, it housed the Sym Choon family and their various enterprises for more than 60 years. Every child had a Sym Choon firecracker. Miss Gladys Sym Choon, purveyor of oriental luxury goods, was the doyenne, and a South Australian institution. Long after Miss Gladys is gone, her name on the shop still has the goods – though now the goods are fashion and textile designs. Further east, the changes wrought by the invention of Frome Street are plain to see. Where Ern Bennetts's barber's pole once rose out of the footpath, is now just footpath.

FLAVEL & SONS LTD., established 1885. General Merchants, 211-215 Rundle Street. Hardware, China, Glass, and Furniture Distributors. Tent and Tarpaulin Manufacturers. Hiring Contractors for the supply of Marquees, Tableing, Seating, etc. Telegraphic and cable address, Phone: C. 2744 (two lines).

THE HOTEL AUSTRAL (W. and Edith M. Garratt), 205 Rundle Street, is a well-known landmark. This Hotel has long been noted for its excellent service in all departments.

HORNER'S CYCLES, 201 Rundle St. New Cycles from £4/10/-. 1 deposit, 2/6 weekly.

M. GASKIN, 199 Rundle Street. Genuine Antiques, Native Weapons, Bronzes, Brasses, Furniture. Antiques of all classes bought. Homes called on. Prompt attention.

HARRY NIMON, Ladies', Gentlemen's, and Children's Draper and Mercer, is at No. 197. Working clothes a speciality.

MALCOLM REID'S Modern Furniture Showrooms are next to Foy's. These fine Showrooms, with their many model furnished rooms, are amongst the most up-to-date in the Commonwealth.

RUNDLE STREET EAST (SOUTH SIDE), BETWEEN BENT STREET AND PULTENEY STREET

AUSTRAL HOTEL (1880s)

MALCOM REID BUILDING (1880s)

The Italianate revival Austral Hotel is the eastern adjunct to a block of 14 sandstone shops that became one when Malcolm Reid & Co. Ltd, "Adelaide's Greatest and Most Spacious Furniture Emporium" moved to the East End a century ago. After a hard day's furniture shopping you could "have your liquid refreshment in comfort and be assured of true hospitality" at the Austral. Today the pub is livelier than that, while Malcolm Reid's "approximately three acres of floor space" and "famous twenty-one Model Furnished rooms" have reverted to the smaller shops, eateries and offices that the South Australian Company intended.

South Australia's Leading Department Store !!

FOY'S

Where Adelaide's "Solid Trading" is done . . . . .

FOR over a quarter century this great store has done service to the people of South Australia . . . a dominating pile which is one of the finest pieces of architectural massiveness in the city to-day, whose flashing dome at night may be seen from foothills to seashore. It is at this store that Adelaide comes for its biggest all-year-round value . . . where trading is more solid than spectacular, where the aim is to give more for the customers' money, and "honest dealing" is the password for every day. Many visitors from the country, interstate, and overseas take away happy memories of their association with Foy's.

Foy's are big buyers of South Australian Wool - - - always have been !!

Foy's are definitely linked with the economic history of South Australia through extensive wool-buying for their Victorian Mills, which incidentally are the largest and best-equipped of their kind this side of the equator. Of the 1935/6 clip alone Foy's purchases in this State exceeded £70,000. This is the wool which goes into the manufacture of the famous "Gibsonia" woollen piece goods and knitted wear . . . recognised as the finest in the Commonwealth and not unknown throughout the whole world.

In this important Centenary Year, Foy's express their great thanks to the South Australian Public for their tremendous support . . . they express a confidence in the future of the State and a hope that each succeeding milestone down the years will continue to see continued peace and prosperity in South Australia . . . land of the wattle.

Foy's always have a warm welcome for Visitors to this State.

FOY & GIBSON PTY. LTD.—RUNDLE AND PULTENEY STREETS, ADELAIDE. C. 5590

RUNDLE STREET EAST (SOUTH SIDE), CORNER OF PULTENEY STREET

The Foy's claim that it was "South Australia's Leading Department Store!!" would be challenged with equal hyperbolic glee by every one of the other big stores up and down what is now Rundle Mall. What the rest didn't have though, was the great Victorian style Foy's premises, originally the Grand Central Hotel. There was nothing else like Foy's in Adelaide and then none at all when the wrecking ball went through it in 1976. Up went a multi-storey car park, which now moonlights as the Rundle Lantern. At night the Lantern draws crowds with its LED-powered moving imagery. Foy's had a commanding elegance around the clock.

CURRIE STREET

COLONEL LIGHT'S MONUMENT

AUSTRALASIAN SCALE CO. LTD., 122-124 Currie St. The home in South Australia of "AVERY" and "ASCO" Weighing Appliances. Phone C. 6244.

CURRIE STREET (NORTH SIDE), BETWEEN LIGHT SQUARE AND KINGSTON STREET

TAFE CAMPUS

GILLINGHAM PRINTERS (1907)

THE HASSELL PRESS (1885)

Adelaide's surveyor, Colonel William Light, is commemorated by a mounted theodolite in the city square named after him. The Colonel himself lies below, the only body known to be buried within Adelaide's square mile. In the centenary year, pilgrims turned up at Light's grave to mark the anniversary of his demise. In later years the Colonel has been kept company in the monumental sense by the writer and suffragette Catherine Helen Spence.

Baring obviously wasn't afraid of competition from other printers. Along this strip, window shopping at Gillingham's and The Hassell Press was allowed. Narrow frontages more than likely saved several small Victorian and Georgian buildings from development later in the 20th century, although the Adelaide City TAFE Campus took out an entire precinct. How quickly the Adelaide CBD changed its moods is illustrated here. Just up the street to the east was the big boardroom end of town – Adelaide Steamship, Elders, the banks. Here motorists stopped for their retreads, or to take the wrecker's shilling. Or they could walk across Currie Street to buy a cow milking machine.

DUKE OF YORK HOTEL (1883)

THE BROADWAY PARKING STATION
for Safe Parking, 64 Currie St.,
caters specially for business men,
country visitors and shoppers.
Centrally situated. Cars washed,
greased, etc. Petrol and oils stocked.

DALGETY'S OFFICES (1918)

A.M. BICKFORD (1880)

KINGSTON STREET

LEIGH STREET

PEEL STREET

CURRIE STREET (NORTH SIDE), BETWEEN KINGSTON STREET AND PEEL STREET

An independent photograph from the same year *Progressive Adelaide* was published clearly shows a white two storey ladies and gents hairdresser next to the Broadway Parking Station. Apparently the barber in question did not respond to the publisher's offer, and so suffered a shave of his own. Bickford's dispensed the best lime cordial under the sun from 44 Currie Street for around 75 years. They also sold sarsaparilla, coconut oil, Sal Vital health salts, eucalyptus oil and their equally famous coffee and chicory essence. Today the building houses an architectural practice and, behind that, State Records.

PEEL STREET

GILBERT PLACE

KING WILLIAM STREET

CURRIE STREET (NORTH SIDE), BETWEEN PEEL STREET AND KING WILLIAM STREET

30 CURRIE STREET   **FORMER BANK OF VICTORIA** (1924)   **FORMER BENNETT AND FISHER BUILDING** (1962)

Where Unity and Davenport Chambers were, the Post Modern detail of 30 Currie Street makes it one of the city's more distinctive office towers. Remarkably, the remnant former bank building next door has always appeared as though a third of it is missing. This end of Currie Street was where most of South Australia's big business decisions were made. While the Great Depression still lingered when the photograph opposite was taken in around 1936, the vigorous architecture here echoed a past period of self-confidence that would return by the 1950s. Stock firm Bennett and Fisher, for one, needed to enlarge its city premises.

ELDER, SMITH & CO., LIMITED.
Founded 1839. Wool and Produce
Brokers, Livestock, Land and Property
Salesmen, General Merchants,
Shipping and Insurance Agents. 27-31
Currie Street, Adelaide. Telephone
Central 3001 (10 lines).

ALFRED CHAMBERS   **ADELAIDE STEAMSHIP COMPANY**

TOPHAM MALL

CURRIE STREET (SOUTH SIDE), BETWEEN KING WILLIAM STREET AND TOPHAM MALL

WESTPAC HOUSE   **FORMER SAVINGS BANK OF**   **ELDER HOUSE** (1937)
                           SOUTH AUSTRALIA (1904)

Side by side, the old Savings Bank head office and Elder House are two of the most significant buildings in Adelaide. Although only the ornate facade of the Savings Bank remains, the Pyrmont stone pair reflects the financial, pastoral and mining foundations of the young colony and State. The eye-catching Adelaide Steamship Company building in the 1936 photo made it a trio by adding transport to that portfolio, until it gave way to the State Bank building, now Westpac House, behind it. Adelaide lost an imposing building in near original condition. The Federal Government rates the Adelaide Steamship building as "destroyed".

COLTON, PALMER & PRESTON

THOMAS HARDY & SONS LTD.

TOPHAM MALL

BLOOR COURT

CURRIE STREET (SOUTH SIDE), BETWEEN TOPHAM MALL AND BLOOR COURT

The Savings Bank of South Australia's first loan was made in 1848 to a young John Colton, who went on to become Premier. He also founded Colton, Palmer & Preston, who made most things that opened and shut, and sold them out of a store that extended south to Waymouth Street. After World War II the firm made Ezy-built, a South Australian clone of the Meccano children's toy construction set. It also created one of Australia's first alarm clocks. The winemaker Thomas Hardy & Sons had premises around Adelaide and at McLaren Vale. The building here was the champagne depot.

CURRIE STREET (SOUTH SIDE), BETWEEN BLOOR COURT AND LIGHT SQUARE

FORMER AVIATION HOUSE (1925)   QUEENS THEATRE (1841)

Aviation House, at 101 Currie, burnt down three years after it was completed, when the *Register* described it as "one of the finest in Australia". So it was rebuilt for the Richards family, who started making motor bodies four years before Holden did. H.C. Richards Ltd was a forerunner of Chrysler Australia. Later the Government bureaucracies moved in, including the Civil Aviation Authority and the Department of Labour. Baby boomers may recall doing their career-defining vocational guidance assessments there. Only one theatre in Australia, in Hobart, is older than the Queen's down Gilles Arcade. Also known as the Old Victoria, it opened with *Othello* in 1841. In the centenary year the Queen's was a car workshop and showroom for the Gilles Arcade Parking Service. It returned to the limelight in 1996 with *The Magic Flute*. Always there, routinely ignored and saved at first almost by accident, the Queen's is now a national treasure.

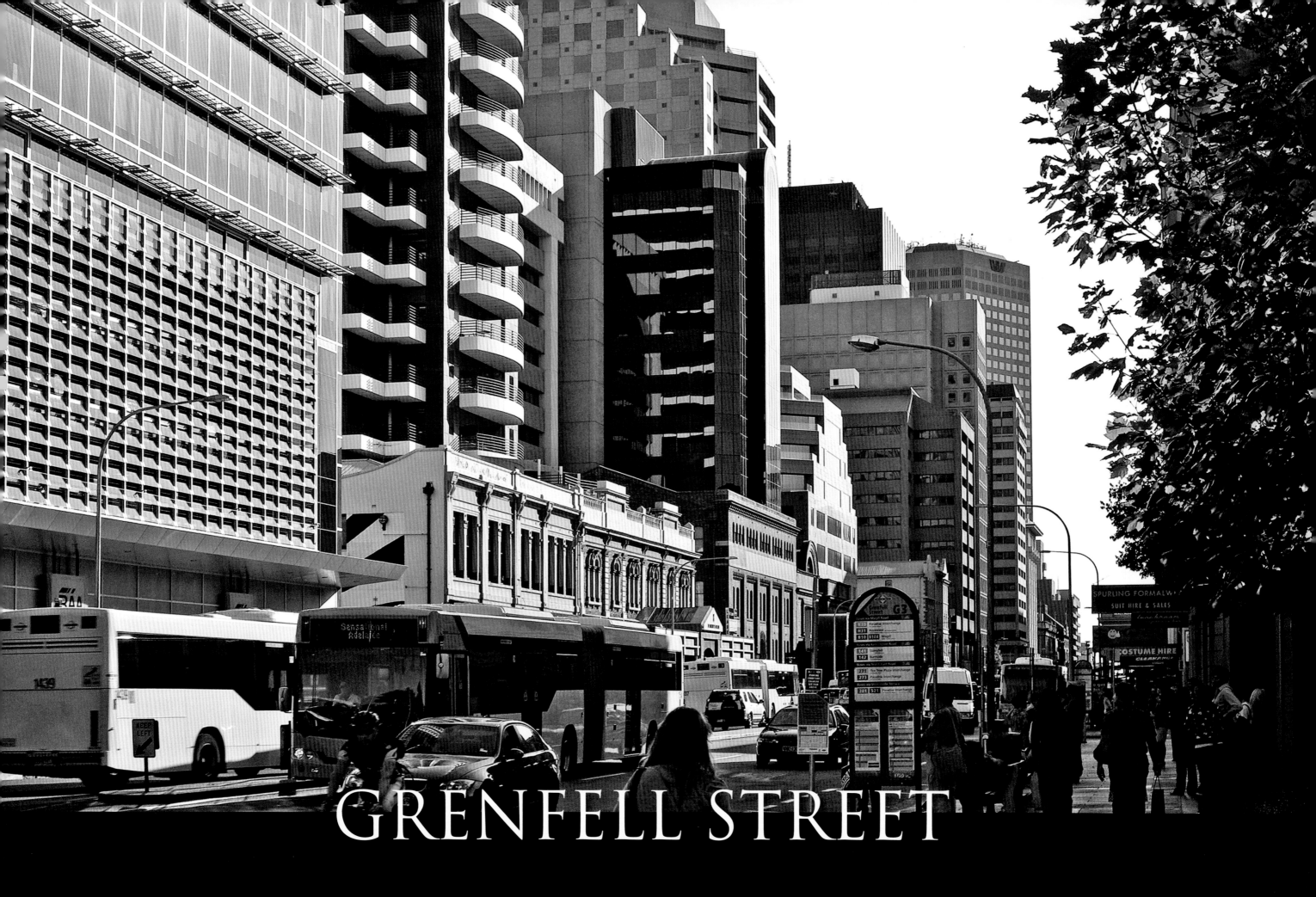

GRENFELL STREET

TATTERSALLS CHAMBERS (1917)
COPYING OFFICE—Misses
M. and E. Furner, 4th floor.
Established 35 years.
J.C. RUNDLE & CO.,
Hotel Brokers and Valuators.
Established 34 years.
Central 1000.

RIGBY LTD

**THE COMMONWEALTH
LIFE (AMALGAMATED)
ASSURANCES LIMITED**
20 Grenfell Street.

ALLIANCE BUILDING (1927)

**SOCIETY FOR THE
PREVENTION OF
CRUELTY TO ANIMALS
INC.** 22 Grenfell Street.

**EXECUTOR TRUSTEE
BUILDING** (1923)

DOBBIE & AMSBERG,
Mercantile Brokers and
Commission Agents.
Kalimna Chambers,
28 Grenfell Street.
Central 4820.

**WIDOWS' FUND BUILDING
MACDOUGALLS LTD**. Importers
& distributors of modern office
machines. Phone: C.1467.
L.C. Smith Typewriters,
Corona Typewriters, Gestetner
Duplicators, Marchant
Calculators, Victor adding
Machines, Dictaphones, Public

Stenographers and Repair
Experts available all hours.
GENERAL ENGRAVERS, H.A.
Pearce, E.L. Churcher, third
floor, Central 2300. **MISS F.
HEWITT** (Confidential Typiste).
First Floor. **WRAY & TUCKER**,
Stock, Share, and Investment
Brokers, 40 Grenfell St. C 64.

J.B. HARRISON & CO. LTD.
Our Business: We Buy, We Sell,
We Value, We Auction and
We Satisfy. Inspect our genuine
values of new and secondhand
furniture at our Sales rooms.
Auctions conducted at shortest
notice with prompt settlements.
46 Grenfell St. Phone: C. 3500.

C.W. OTTAWAY & CO.,
Jewellers, Silversmiths. Importers
of fine china. High-class fancy
goods. Specimen precious
stone, black opals, etc.   **Y.M.C.A.**

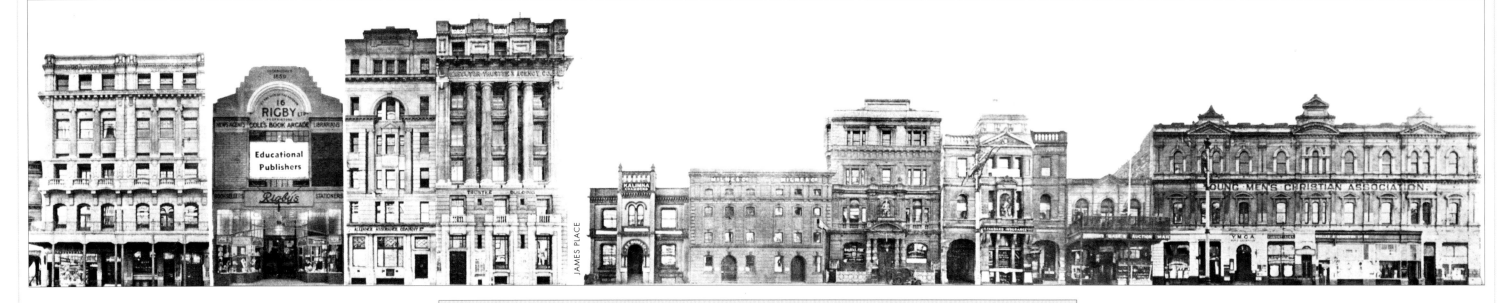

GRENFELL STREET (NORTH SIDE), BETWEEN KING WILLIAM STREET AND GAWLER PLACE

TATTERSALLS CLUB

**FORMER EAGLE STAR
INSURANCE BUILDING**

CITY CROSS

The Tattersalls Club has all the ambience of a past Adelaide sporting life – horseshoes on the balustrades, phone cubicles for betting, a shoeshine machine for the dapper gentleman gambler, a lovely long timber bar for him to lean on. Everything about the Tatts Club is original, just waiting for starter's orders again. Where there's a quid, there's a way. Resourceful Baring fell big time for Rigby's when the venerable South Australian bookseller took out a full page ad in *Progressive Adelaide*. So he gave Rigby's a larger, wider, taller building alongside the Tatts Club – but the camera never lies in Mick Bradley's photo. The upstanding Alliance and Executor Trustee buildings next door exude commercial confidence and security to this day, while the 1960s former Eagle Star Insurance tower is well regarded for its crisp post war International style. Architects still carry a torch for it. In the Widows' Fund Building, in the vicinity of today's City Cross, Miss F. Hewitt carved out a career as a Confidential Typiste, duplicating and multigraphing before the computer age. Further along, young men fresh off the boats and trains and buckboards found their "Ideal Home" at the clean-living Y. These days you go to that address for your liquor and gambling licences.

THEODORE BRUCE & CO. Established over 50 years. Land, Furniture, Art, and Machinery, Auctioneers and Valuators. Telephone: Central 820. 70a Grenfell Street, situated next to Harris Scarfe Ltd. Furniture purchased outright. Always a large quantity of furniture for private sale. Prompt account sales.

HOLDEN & FROST BUILDING

EVANS & CLARKE Adelaide's leading auctioneers and valuators of Property, Furniture, Machinery, Drapery, Groceries, Motor Cars, and General Merchandise. Large and commodious auction and private salesrooms. 98-100 Grenfell Street. Crowds of buyers always attend our popular auction sales.

The Ballroom Magnificent **"EMBASSY"** Adelaide's Luxurious Ballroom. Direction: J. Morris. Phone: C. 5566.

STURT ARCADE HOTEL (Mrs M.E. Whallin, Proprietress) Grenfell Street. Dinners specially catered for. A Modern Lounge. Hot and cold water in all rooms. Phone: C. 7295

GRENFELL STREET (NORTH SIDE), BETWEEN GAWLER PLACE AND ARCADE LANE

DA COSTA BUILDING

HARRIS SCARFE BUILDING
(demolished 2011)

GRENFELL CARPARK

Da Costa Building was named after the philanthropist Benjamin Mendes da Costa, who lived on the corner and left the real estate to St Peter's College. Harris Scarfe set up shop here in 1877 as Geo. P. Harris, Scarfe & Co. The South Australian retail institution's main presence later shifted north through the city block to the sexier Rundle Mall, but both familiar faces are gone now. Plenty of Holdens are parked in Grenfell Carpark. So it's fitting that they are suspended in and above the space where the Holden family made their first fortune in saddlery and coachbuilding, and where the young Edward Holden first played with motorcars.

GRENFELL STREET (NORTH SIDE), BETWEEN ARCADE LANE AND HINDMARSH SQUARE

Irishman John Galligan was a great mattress maker, not so good a businessman. Legend has it that he struck gold in Kalgoorlie after selling out to the McCarthy family. At the Grenfell Street store, where the clowns are now, Galligans became unofficial mattress supplier to South Australia. Their slogan "The Secret of Sleep!" gave way to the indestructible "Say Goodnight Galligans!" Owner Jeff McCarthy can reveal that the voiceover culprit is Ugly Dave Gray, the '70s TV comedian. International Business Machines would become the world's biggest computer company, as IBM. In Adelaide it was content with a shopfront in the sturdy bluestone Hindmarsh Buildings, along with Gray & Palmer, purveyors of McKee's Brilliantine.

GRENFELL STREET (NORTH SIDE), BETWEEN FROME STREET AND EAST TERRACE

When the Adelaide Produce Market moved out of the city a generation ago, the old Fruit and Produce Exchange became prime residential real estate. Now many prominent citizens reside behind a facade. But with its ornamental and exuberant sentiments the facade complements both the quiet lives behind it, and the nightlife that surrounds it.

ADELAIDE ELECTRIC SUPPLY COMPANY

PRODUCERS' CLUB HOTEL, 235 Grenfell St. John J. Dunn, Proprietor. Good accommodation, moderate Tariff, ideal situation. Close to Botanic Gardens, etc. Phone: C. 2871.

O.F. SPEHR, Potato and Onion Specialist. 233 Grenfell Street. Seed lines in stock. Goods forwarded to all parts of the State. Phone: C. 4704.

GRENFELL STREET (SOUTH SIDE), CORNER OF EAST TERRACE

GRENFELL STREET (SOUTH SIDE), BETWEEN TAM O'SHANTER PLACE AND FROME STREET

TAM O'SHANTER PLACE

TANDANYA NATIONAL CULTURAL INSTITUTE

OLD EXCHANGE HOTEL (1904)

Builders found tonnes of coal and an undocumented void when they recycled Adelaide's first major powerhouse. Since 1923 the Grenfell Street Power Station blew black smoke in the city's face at the same time as it illuminated the streets and rattled the trams. Its other saving grace was its commanding architecture. Today as Tandanya National Aboriginal Cultural Institute, the old power station radiates the creative energy generated by the art and performance of Aboriginal and Torres Strait Islander Australians. Tandanya means "place of the red kangaroo" in the Kaurna language of the first people of the Adelaide Plains. The hotel next door has had several names, usually more than once. It started in 1839 as the Woodman Inn, and was again 150 years later. It was the Electric Light when the power station came along, and was again not long ago. In between it was the Producers, or Producers' Club. Now it is the Old Exchange, after the former Fruit and Produce Exchange across Grenfell Street. Like that Exchange, the hotel is still a looker, which is exactly as the brewery architects intended.

WML MANURES

THE FORMER CONGREGATIONAL CHURCH

GRENFELL STREET (SOUTH SIDE), BETWEEN FROME STREET AND HINDMARSH SQUARE

FROME STREET

Adelaide already was dedicated to the car in the 1930s, and the truck, although not in every driveway, was the 4WD of its day. Horses are much greener than the internal combustion engine, however. Their emissions still sold well for recycling back then. Remember, "it pays to fertilise with WML high grade manures". Until the Australian Broadcasting Commission bolted for the suburbs in the mid 1970s, its Adelaide home was the former Congregational Church on a corner of Grenfell Street and Hindmarsh Square. At some stage in between, the twin stone belltowers were removed to give Broadcast House a more secular look. These were the golden years of radio, and the ABC was right there in the thick of it.

Hindmarsh Square, Adelaide

FORMER YWCA BUILDING (1900)

These days, it is not the done thing to criticise trams. They are cleaner and quieter than buses. Adelaide once was full of trams. It was a big mistake to get rid of them between then and now. Yet they had their detractors in the past. The socialist city councillor Frank Lundie railed against the way trams encroached on the city squares. Here in Hindmarsh Square you can see why. The Royal Automobile Association came to the aid of motorists where, fittingly, a "green" apartment building and office now stands. The RAA maintains its presence at street level. Next door, the former YWCA building still stands sentinel.

MOTORISTS ORGANISE
join the
for PROTECTION SAVINGS SERVICE.

HARRISON SAN MIGUEL PTY. LTD., 131 Grenfell Street. Manufacturers and Suppliers.

EDINA KNITTING MILLS (E. Hosking, Proprietor), established 1923. Specialising in tailored knitwear, coats, frocks, jerseys, dressing gowns. Home knitwear carefully brushed by experts. Phone: C. 3211.

J.N. TAYLOR & CO. LTD., Well-known city merchant house, established 1887. General soft goods, woollens, trimmings. Motor cycles, cycles, spare parts, accessories for cars and trucks. Makers of Taylor Pistons for internal combustion engines. Phone: 6710 (4 Lines).

WYATT HOUSE MOTORS, LTD., Agents for A.J.S. Motor Cycles, Radio, Refrigerators, Push Cycles, Accessories, Oil and Petrol. Phone: C. 8620. **NOEL H. HUBBLE'S PHYSICAL CULTURE & DANCING COLLEGE**. Established 16 years. All branches of Physical Culture and Gymnastics for Ladies, Gentlemen, and Children. Special department for remedial cases. Phone: C. 3625.

H.S. SLOMAN LIMITED, Wholesale and Retail Merchants, specialising in Car & Truck accessories and replacement parts, cycles, engineers tools, hardware, and gentlemen's footwear. Phone: C. 4993.

T.C. HUNTER, Furrier, Dresser, and Dyer of all Furred Skins. Furs cleaned, renovated and remodelled. Furs, Fur Coats, Rugs, etc., of all descriptions. A good range always stocked. Phone: C. 1963.

GRENFELL STREET (SOUTH SIDE), BETWEEN HINDMARSH SQUARE AND WYATT STREET

FORMER WYATT HOUSE

In the late 1980s the National Trust fought for the retention of historical frontages along Grenfell Street. Facadism is often dismissed, but is it better than the complete loss of historical character? Here, what was Wyatt House is a good place for you to judge for yourself.

WILKINSON & CO., Viceroy Tea. 107-105 Grenfell Street.

J.W. GRASBY & CO. LTD. Wholesale grocers and importers, 97 Grenfell Street.

BICKERSTAFF & SCOTT LTD. Manufacturers' and Importers Agents, 91 Grenfell Street.

WORANDO BUILDING McLEAY BROS. LTD. Wholesale and Retail Furniture. Phone: C. 3791. **HAROLD GORDON**, Distributing Semco Products (wholesale only). C. 2919. No.17, Third Floor, are **BRIGINSHAW BROTHERS**, Manufacturing Specialists. Marking Tickets, Tags, Labels, Staples, Display Clips, Pins, Cash Register Rolls. Phone: C. 2659. **S. HOFFNUNG & CO. LTD.** Distributors H.M.V., Columbia, Parlophone Records; H.M.V. Radio; Wahl-Eversharp Pens, Pencils; Gem Razors; Ever-Ready Batteries; Straitline Cartridges, etc. **HENRY SAVAGE & SONS LTD.** Warehousemen. **SAVSON SOFTGOODS**, established 1902. Phone: C. 596. **HOWARD C. MICKLEM**, Central 2479. Established 1923. Box 377. **MERCANTILE AGENCIES LIMITED,** Manufacturers' Agents and Brokers, 3rd floor. Phone: C. 7673. Phone: 1485L. **E. BOWN.** **MISS ELSIE DOBSON**, Photographic Artist and Retoucher. Phone: C. 2659. **MISS GEDGE, SOFT FURNISHINGS** (Trade only), 4th floor. Phone: C. 2716.

GRENFELL STREET (SOUTH SIDE), BETWEEN WYATT STREET AND GAWLER PLACE

You feel as though you only have to scrape away the filling to expose again Wilkinson & Co., the home of "100% British Empire Grown" Viceroy Tea and Arab Brand Groceries. The Viceroy ad said "Every man, woman & child in South Aust. drinks on the average 5 cups of tea a day". No wonder the Empire was still a going concern in 1936. Later, the building was nicely recycled as the Mail Exchange. Now it's a facade. Tucked around the corner in Chesser Street at the back of Bickerstaff & Scott was Baring Printers, where *Progressive Adelaide* was made. Today it is a staff training room in a high rise behind a facade with post-modern flourishes. Then it was a hive of activity, with most of the men wearing bow ties so as not to be strangled – or worse – in the highly mechanised pre-computer printing process.

FORMER WILKINSON & CO. BUILDING
(1898)

**BRITISH AND FOREIGN
BIBLE SOCIETY**

COROMANDEL PLACE

GAWLER PLACE

A. NOBLE & SON.—Established 1911—Engineering, Mining, and Foundry Specialists, occupy the premises at 79 Grenfell Street. These premises—which extend from the Grenfell Street frontage to French Street at the rear, were at one time owned by the South Australian Gas Company.

A.W. SANDFORD & CO. LIMITED, 75 Grenfell Street, Produce and General Merchants, Established 1874.

BRITISH AND FOREIGN BIBLE SOCIETY, South Australia Auxiliary, Incorporated, 73 Grenfell Street.

ADELAIDE BUSINESS COLLEGE—Roneo House, 69 Grenfell St. Phone: C 8095.

A. MURDOCH & CO. LTD. Merchants, Manufacturers' Agents and warehouse. 63 Grenfell St. C 7044. Verandah Blinds be prepared for the summer, consult A. Murdoch & Co. Ltd.

GRENFELL STREET (SOUTH SIDE), BETWEEN WYATT STREET AND GAWLER PLACE

BERTRAM HOUSE
(1898)

A tower and podium stands where McLeay Bros "The Value First Furnishers" traded in the Worando Building, barely an em-rule away from Baring Printers. McLeay's famous slogan was "Buy direct and bank the difference". Could the multi-skilled Hermann Baring have invented it? That's possible, say Travis and Robin McLeay today. No one else has claimed the honour, and it is known that Barings printed for McLeays. Or could it have been Hermann's tenant Les J. Kyte, Adelaide's ad man extraordinaire? Parts of the south side of Grenfell Street have been gutted for high rise, but nobody has messed with Bertram House, and just as well. Once owned by the British and Foreign Bible Society, the classic little red brick Gothic building has rare 19th century polished timberwork inside. It's a crowd favourite, and would make a statement for a pedestrian cafe precinct behind it.

ADELAIDE DEVELOPMENT CO. BUILDINGS. *Progress in Australia.* South Australia's Leading Magazine. An independent review of Australian Travel, Art, Industry, Politics, and Commerce. Published monthly by **PROGRESS PUBLISHING COMPANY LTD.** 55 Grenfell St. Phone: C. 513. **HOLDSWORTH & CO. LTD.,** Imperial Typewriters Agents, Phone: C.1100.

L. WIENER—TAILOR, 51 Grenfell St. C. 1925. **W.M. BEAVEN & SON,** Shoe Manufacturers' Agents and Warehousemen. C. 1688. **CHERITON & RASHLEIGH,** Licensed Land Brokers, Financiers, & Estate Agents. C. 8844. **LIMBERTS RADIO SHOWROOMS,** 49a Grenfell St. C. 1136. All classes of Radio. Technical service. **THE "VANDERBILT"** most modernly equipped Milk Bar. Courtesy, efficiency. C. 2811.

GRENFELL BUILDING
THE A.J. QUARRELL ADVERTISING SERVICE, (Basement), Service and General Advertising. **EDWIN H. CROPLEY,** F.R.E.I. Est. 1905. Land & Estate Agent. **GOODE, DURRANT & MURRAY LTD.** Telegrams, "Tenomis, Adelaide." Also at London, Paris, Perth, Broken Hill, Sydney and New York. Agency at Melbourne. C 6600.

BROOKMAN BUILDINGS
T.M. BURKE PTY. LTD., Land & Estate Agents. P.O. Box 753F. C. 6040. **CHARLES F. ADAMS,** Estate and Financial Agent. 120, fourth floor. C. 8434. **WERE'S MERCANTILE AGENCY LTD.** (formerly R.G. Dun & Co. in S.A., Est.1842). C. 5695. **E. PHILLIPPS DANKER** Architect, Vice-Consul for Spain. C. 3433.

F. MULLER, Diamond Setter and Ring Maker. Top floor Cavendish Chambers.

CHARTRES LTD., Remington Typewriters. Central 8283 (four lines). Representing Remington for 50 years. **CHARTRES BUSINESS COLLEGE.**

COWRA CHAMBERS
COPYING OFFICE. Adelaide Typewriting Association (Miss K. Hardy). Typewriting, multigraphing, duplicating. All classes of circularising undertaken. 8 Cowra Chambers. Phone: C. 1109. **SMITH'S WEEKLY** (The People's Guardian). **THE REFEREE** (50 years of world's sport).

HOTEL BROKERS, O.H. DUHST & CO. Licensed Land Agents. Royal Insurance Building.

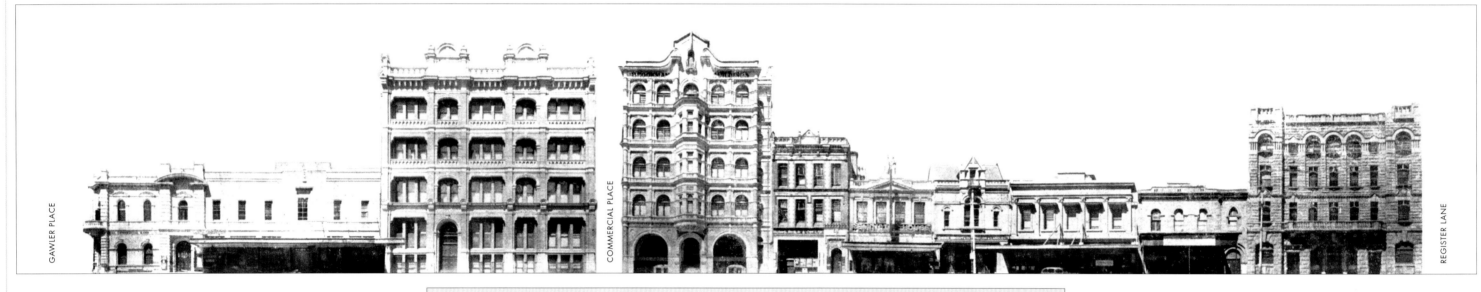

GAWLER PLACE · COMMERCIAL PLACE · REGISTER LANE

GRENFELL STREET (SOUTH SIDE), BETWEEN GAWLER PLACE AND REGISTER LANE

GRENFELL CENTRE

Here, an appealing variety of buildings has been replaced by a cacophony in pre-stressed concrete. That's progress. The Adelaide Development Co., with offices along here, knew all about progress when it declared "the paddocks of today will be the suburbs of tomorrow". Too right! The ADC is still around, with properties in the CBD. Along with the Vice-Consul for Spain, the Adelaide office of *Smith's Weekly* or "The People's Guardian", the campaigning tabloid that entertained Australia for 30 years, was around about where the "Black Stump", aka the Grenfell Centre, is now. Right alongside today's Stump at No. 25, for many years the large gold letters on a window at No. 23 read "Don Bradman and Co." The greatest cricketer of them all was a canny businessman. His sharebroking and investment firm waited at the end of the eastern suburbs tram line. That meant well-off middle-class city workers were reminded of The Don and his services every working morning and night. It is said that Don Bradman's marketing was almost as efficacious as his batting.

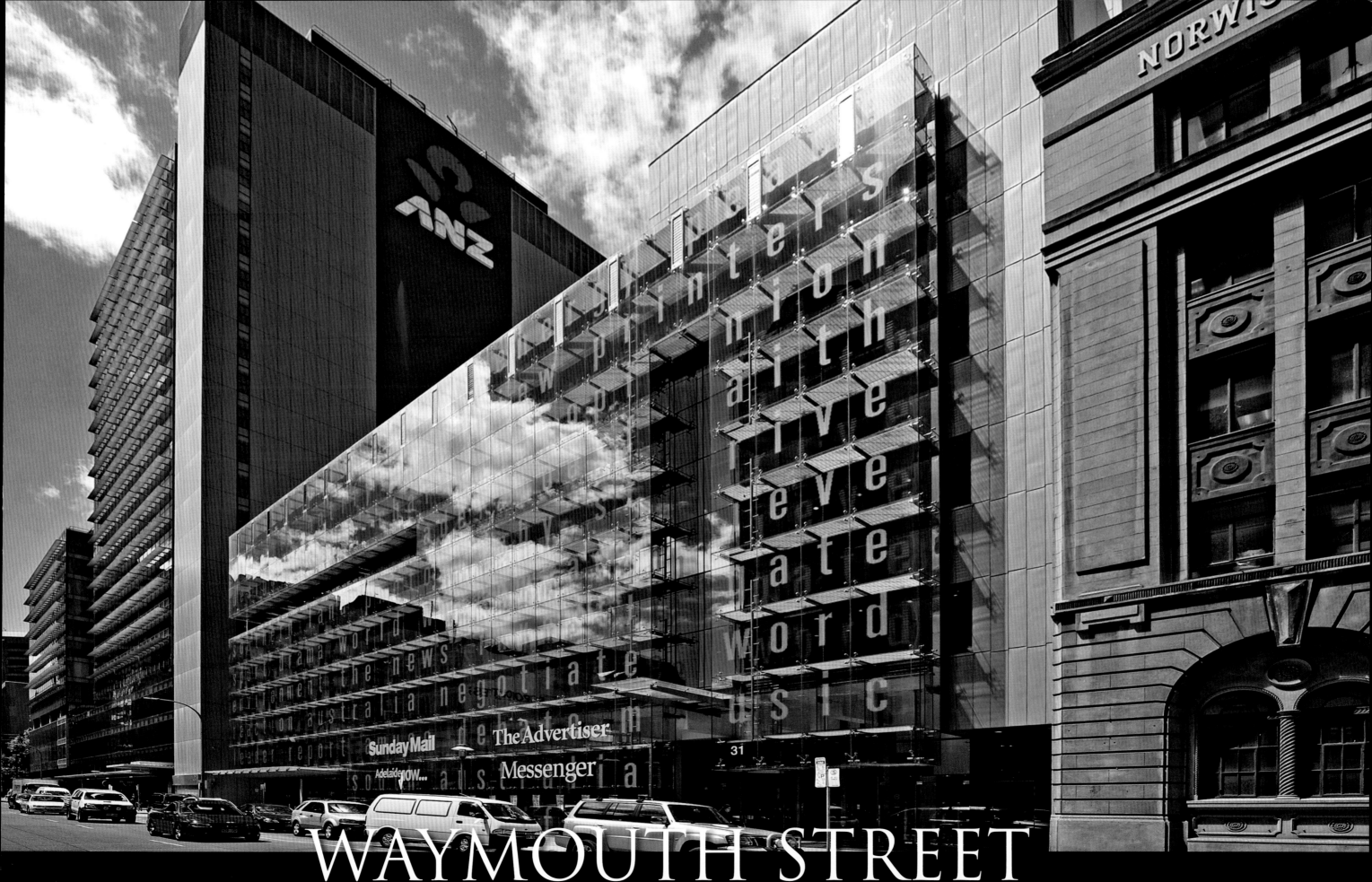

WAYMOUTH STREET

T.L. BUILDINGS. PAPER PRODUCTS
LIMITED. Paper & Board converters.

WAYMOUTH STREET (NORTH SIDE), BETWEEN LIGHT SQUARE AND YOUNG STREET

WAREHOUSE (1880, demolished in 2011)

One firm dominated this part of Waymouth Street in 1936. McPherson's WAS machinery in Adelaide 75 years ago – "Australia's leading engineering supply house" – an ironmonger's reverie. Today a courtyard and plaza are on the way. Mick Bradley's camera captured the fine old warehouse on the Light Square corner soon before it was turned to dust. Meanwhile, across the square the former Sands & McDougall warehouse has been given a new life as affordable housing.

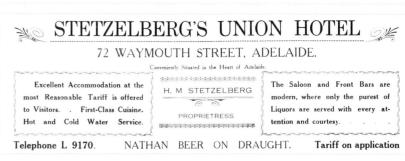
TOLLEY WAREHOUSE (1913)   **ROYAL MAIL STABLES**   **UNION HOTEL** (1880)

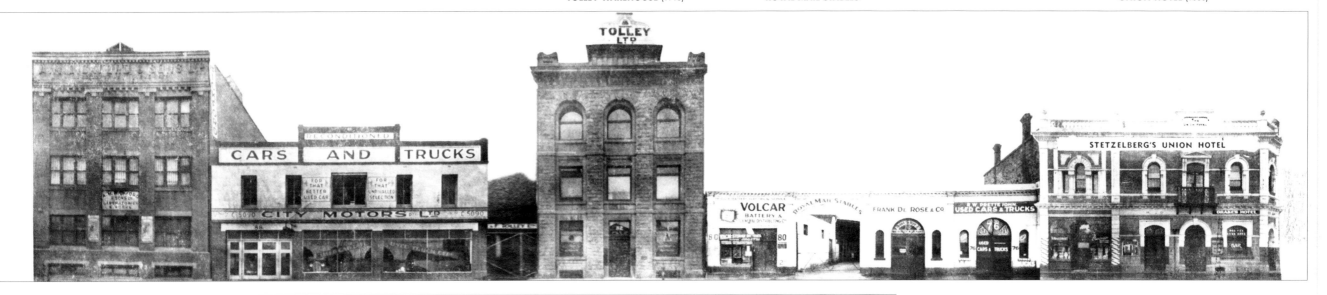

WAYMOUTH STREET (NORTH SIDE), BETWEEN YOUNG STREET AND UNION HOTEL

The robust industrial Tolley warehouse has lost its rendered ground floor windowsills on both sides, but it and its street still get along well. Pity the Royal Mail stables had to go though. They were worth keeping for the romance alone. The Union Hotel once had a black tiger. Later it was the newspaperman's after-hours consolation for a life worked upside down. Now it buzzes along a nightclub strip that would have been considered unlikely on Waymouth Street only a few years ago. Media people still work the street, and the Union.

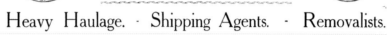

WAYMOUTH STREET (NORTH SIDE), BETWEEN UNION HOTEL AND WAYMOUTH PLACE

By comparison, this streetscape fared better than its mirror image Pirie Street on the other side of King William Street. The building retention rate along here is relatively high, which could explain why it has grown in the public's affection. Dining and nightlife entrepreneurs have managed to find atmospheric locations for bars, cafes and restaurants. Adelaide's "party precinct", as it is now known, starts here and swings west along Waymouth.

FIRE
MOTORS
WORKMEN
and
ALL CLASSES
of
AGRICULTURAL
and
GENERAL
INSURANCE

IN EVERY TOWN AN AGENT
The **C·I·C**
IN EVERY AGENT A FRIEND

The Co-operative Insurance Coy. of Aust. Ltd.
Co-operative Insurance House, Bentham Street (off Waymouth Street). Look for C.I.C. Clock.

SOUTH AUSTRALIAN GAS COMPANY

NORWICH FIRE INSURANCE (1929)

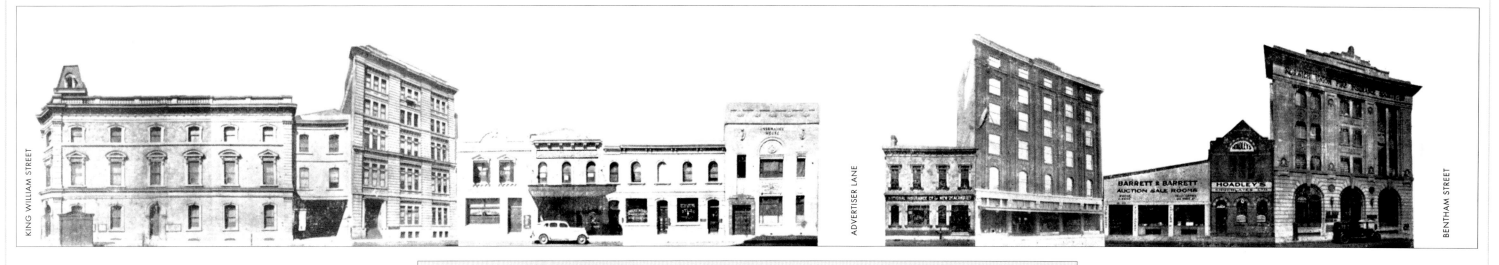

KING WILLIAM STREET

ADVERTISER LANE

BENTHAM STREET

WAYMOUTH STREET (SOUTH SIDE), BETWEEN KING WILLIAM STREET AND BENTHAM STREET

KEITH MURDOCH HOUSE

This used to be one of the few remaining industrial precincts in the centre of town. At night, the *Advertiser*'s printing presses rumbled in a building that looked like boom-time Chicago. Students gathered in Advertiser Lane for the exam results that would determine their lives. South Australians bought their stoves from "the Gas Company". Now all is modern glass except for the fine old Norwich Fire Insurance building on the far corner. The *Advertiser*'s triple-glazed Keith Murdoch House memorialises the man who told the world the story of Gallipoli and the Anzacs.

TRANSPORT SPECIALISTS

NASH CARS
Famous for quality at reasonable price. Available in four distinct sizes.

FEDERAL TRUCKS
From ¾ ton to 10 tons and truck construction throughout.

GARDNER DIESEL ENGINES
For conversion of petrol trucks. Save of 80 per cent. fuel costs as compared to petrol.

H.S.C.S. DIESEL TRACTORS
Creeper and Wheel Types for farm and industrial purposes.

DIESEL REPAIRS
As Gardner Diesel Engine Distributors we have built up a technical staff of trained men for repairs and servicing.

Maintaining a sound growth by marketing reliable units we have built up a comprehensive Motor Business which includes the sale of Used Cars and Trucks, Mechanical Service and the agencies mentioned in the margin.

Rasch Motors Ltd. 59-63 Waymouth St., ADELAIDE 'Phone: Central 8071

THISTLE HOTEL

LAYCOCK'S MONUMENTAL AND MARBLE WORKS, etc. (H. Simmons, Proprietor). Head Office and Works: 81 Waymouth St. Also Main North Road. Phone C. 1581. After hours: M 1692.

There is money in Angora Rabbits.

WAYMOUTH STREET (SOUTH SIDE), BETWEEN BENTHAM STREET AND YOUNG STREET

AUSTRALIAN TAXATION OFFICE

Even when the city was generously endowed with pubs, the Thistle on the corner was one of Adelaide's more endearing little hotels. Now it is five-star, European-style luxury. Next door is another one of the CBD's miniature anomalies – a site either too dinky to develop or too stubborn to succumb. The tax office gives this section of the street a certain gravitas it lacked when it was warehousing and an outlet for all that Motor City USA had to offer. On this page and elsewhere in *Progressive Adelaide*, Baring urged farming angora rabbits for their silky wool as a pathway to prosperity in South Australia. "There is money in Angora Rabbits", he declared, showing how astute investment could be multiplied 10-fold if you had the right doe. It never caught on in a big way, however, probably because of the high cost of shearing rabbits.

F.C. PENGILLY, 9 Young Street, Motor Body and Lorry Builder and General Repairer. Trimming and Painting. Established 1900.

FOX MOTOR CO., 103 Waymouth St. Adelaide's leading dealer in modern and genuinely low-mileaged used cars. We have always an exclusive range for immediate demonstration and delivery. Liberal allowance on your present car. Phone: C. 4906. "For Exclusive Used Cars."

P. PANOS, 107 Waymouth St., Confectionery, Cool Drinks, Cigarettes, and Tobacco.

LORD RAGLAN HOTEL (Harry Bailey), 109 Waymouth St.

WAYMOUTH STREET (SOUTH SIDE), BETWEEN YOUNG STREET AND CANNON STREET

FEDERATION TRADING BUILDING (1866)

The bluestone and red brick Federation Trading building always has stood out in its quiet, colonial way. It was purpose built to make the 19th century baking sensation, aerated bread, which used carbon dioxide instead of yeast to give a loaf a rise. Machinery-made, "no sweat!" bread, ran one glowing endorsement.

WAYMOUTH STREET (SOUTH SIDE), BETWEEN TATHAM STREET AND LIGHT SQUARE

LIGHT BUILDINGS   FORMER T. TALBOT, LATER STORMY'S

The shopfront address of T. Talbot, a humble motor painter and trimmer down near Light Square, would one day be given the monumental lobby and stairwell treatment. It became the home business of Adelaide's most famous madam, Stormy Summers, but not before an art deco twinning with the Master Butchers next door to become the attractive Light Buildings. That was soon after Baring came snapping.

PIRIE STREET

ROXY MILK & COFFEE BAR in 1937

MACKENZIE & QUIRKE,
Gentlemen's Outfitters,
are at 4 Manufactures
Place. Phone: C. 3722.

THE RAPID COPYING OFFICE (Miss A.
Spilsbury) is at Manufactures Place, Pirie
Street. Phone: C. 1236.

THE MODERN BUSINESS COLLEGE
(Miss A. Spilsbury) is on the third floor.
Expert tuition. Prospectus on application.
Phone: C. 1236

BARRETT & BARRETT, Licensed Land
Brokers and Agents, Auctioneers and
Valuers. All real estate documents
prepared. Valuations made for probate
purposes. Auction sales conducted
on shortest notice. Rents and interest
collected. 28 Pirie Street. Cent. 6655.

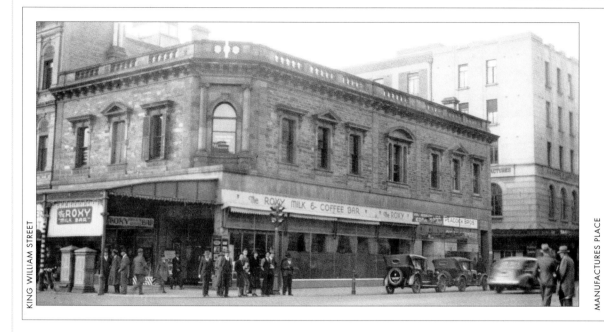

KING WILLIAM STREET

MANUFACTURES PLACE

EXCHANGE PLACE

PIRIE STREET (NORTH SIDE), BETWEEN KING WILLIAM STREET AND GAWLER PLACE

MANUFACTURES PLACE

TELSTRA BUILDING

Down from the Roxy Milk Bar in little Manufactures Place just off Pirie Street, Miss A. Spilsbury ran both The Rapid Copying Office for typewriting, duplicating and multigraphing, and The Modern Business College. When page space was tight, Baring might leave such minor thoroughfares out of the picture. But Manufactures Place remains while every building in its Pirie Street neighbourhood has vanished. The Britannia Statue on top of the building at right was a city sight for around three-quarters of a century. An arm was damaged by an earthquake in 1897, followed by the head in another in 1902. Then the Big Quake of 1954 proved too much for the old girl. She cracked at her base. For the Great Symbol of the Empire, discretion became the better part of valour. Britannia was deposed for the safety of her subjects. Her building made way for Telstra in the 1980s.

HOTEL ADELAIDE

GAWLER PLACE

PIRIE STREET (NORTH SIDE), BETWEEN KING WILLIAM STREET AND GAWLER PLACE

Still missed after 40 years is an early Hotel Adelaide, a genuine charmer. It was also absent from *Progressive Adelaide*. That could be because the scaffolding was up in the centenary year. Until then the hotel was known as the Selborne, birthplace in 1890 of the Working Women's Trade Union. It re-emerged as the art deco Adelaide by 1937. As you can see though, none of these buildings had a hope in the end.

F. BOURNE & SON, 66 Pirie Street, Ladies' Costumiers, Clerical and Military Tailors and Outfitters. First-Class London Diploma. Phone: C. 3783.

W.V. O'GRADY, 68 Pirie St. High Class Hairdresser and Tobacconist. All smokers' requests stocked. Our motto: "Cleanliness."

RADIO SERVICE LIMITED, 74a Pirie Street, Radio Repair Specialists. Also distributors of all leading makes of Radio Receivers. Phone: C. 1101.
JENKINS & PALMER, Mercantile Brokers, 74a Pirie Street. We specialize particularly in Cornsacks, Wheat, Grain, Chaff, etc. also Firewood (wholesale); shippers of Fresh and Dried Fruits. For information ring C. 2131-2.

ANDREWS BROS. PROPRIETARY LIMITED, 76 Pirie Street, (Incorporated in Victoria), Woollen and Manchester Warehousemen. Foremost for selection and service. Phone: C. 736 (two lines).

H.E. SIBLEY & COMPANY LTD., 82 Pirie Street, Motor Spare Parts and Accessory Specialist. Phone: C. 5889.

COLEMAN QUICKLITE CO., 84 Pirie Street, Distributors of Coleman Petrol and Kerosene Lamps and Lanterns, Petrol Irons, Stoves, etc. Phone: C. 5661.

SALVATION ARMY PEOPLE'S PALACE

GAWLER PLACE

COROMANDEL PLACE

CHESSER STREET

PIRIE STREET (NORTH SIDE), BETWEEN GAWLER PLACE AND WYATT STREET

NAB BUILDING

With its clean lines, the NAB building at left is a favourite of architects, while the surviving better half of the late Victorian Italianate sandstone in the middle of the strip is one for the idiosyncratics. It is the only building on the north side of Pirie Street from King William Street to Hindmarsh Square to last until now. More to its credit, someone appears to have made the effort to give it offspring next door. Even an early Salvos' People's Palace in the Venetian Gothic style didn't make the cut.

G. HOLMAN, 104 Pirie Street, specialises in Antiques and Works of Art. Phone C. 7518.

ELLIOT CYCLE STORES have opened here with a large stock of their famous Cycles. 110 Pirie Street.

PHOENIX MOTOR CO., 112 Pirie Street, caters for Repairs, Tyres, Accessories, spare parts, etc. Parking under cover. Phone: C. 2452.

A.L. CAMPBELL & CO. PTY. LTD., 132 Pirie Street, Agents for Ferodo Brake and Clutch Linings, Impregno Case-Hardening Compounds and Crystals. Manufacturers of Camant Brand Polishing Mops and Materials for Electroplaters; Suppliers of Electrical Insulating Materials, etc. Phone: C. 2910.

THE HINDMARSH HOTEL, corner of Hindmarsh Square and Pirie Street, is a well-known landmark. The Proprietress, MRS. B. PIERCE, is always pleased to see old and new friends. WEST END ALES are on draught, and all the best spirits and wines are obtainable. Good accommodation at a reasonable tariff. Phone: C. 5423.

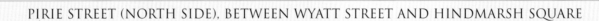

PIRIE STREET (NORTH SIDE), BETWEEN WYATT STREET AND HINDMARSH SQUARE

The east end of Pirie Street was where cars were fixed, starting here. Today it is where they are parked in rows on top of each other. Rather than hiding parked cars, in Europe there is a trend to showing them stacked behind glass, on display. Is that more interesting than a blank wall? Or would it be better to take a walk, ride a bike or catch a tram?

HEALING'S commenced in South Australia in a small way in 1914, having been first established in Melbourne in 1897. Indicative of their progress is the fact that over the last three years they have practically trebled their staff. The home of Healing Golden-Voiced Radio, incorporating all modern devices, but retaining that purity of tone so essential to good receivers. Healing's cater for all Radio and Electrical services, with Radio Receivers, Parts, and Accessories; Modern Home and Office Lighting Fittings; Domestic and Heavy Duty Heating and Cooking Appliances. Their service to the public includes an up-to-date Radio Service Department, and a modern Electrical Workshop. Phone: C. 4633.

CORNER OF PIRIE STREET AND PULTENEY STREET (SOUTH SIDE)

Large public gatherings to enjoy major events in other places are nothing new. These days it is via giant television screens. A.G. Healing Limited, "the 'COMPLETE' Motor, Motorcycle, Cycle, Radio and Electrical Organisation", once had its own version, called "re-diffusion". From *Progressive Adelaide*: "Healing's made history in their re-diffusion of the 1934 series of Test matches in England in search of the historical 'Ashes,' when they showed a replica of the playing field, and each strike scored, by coloured lights. Thousands watched and listened to this re-diffusion from Hindmarsh Square, which faces their building." Valiant as the attempt was, broadcasting by electric light bulb never quite caught on in Adelaide. For their efforts, however, Healing's later scored heavily with their Golden Voice radio and television sets. Fittingly, the site now houses an advertising agency.

147 PIRIE STREET

F.W. MAERSCHEL, Used Car and Truck Specialist, specializing in General Motors' Products, including slightly used latest models. All jobs thoroughly reconditioned before being offered for sale. Personal and confidential attention to all enquiries. Phone: C. 5311.

JOS. A. BISHOP-HALL, Coach and Motor Trimmer, is also in this building. Phone: C. 5736.

C.W. BLANCHARD, Car Painter and Pyroxylin Specialist, is also at this address. Cars painted with lacquer or enamel. Phone: C. 5736.

TED MURPHY, Motor Mechanic, is also at this address. All classes of repairs. Phone: C. 3635.

PERCE A. HARE, Motor Spring Maker, Blacksmith, and Oxywelder, is also in this building. Phone: C. 3635.

SMITH AND DOVE Auto Electrical Engineers. 125-127 Pirie Street.

CENTRAL FURNITURE EXCHANGE PTY. LTD., 121-3 Pirie Street. This is Adelaide's Old-Established Auction Mart, where you can BUY, SELL, or EXCHANGE furniture and all household goods. Auctions or Valuations conducted throughout the State. Phone: C. 3559.

PIRIE STREET (SOUTH SIDE), BETWEEN NAYLOR STREET AND WYATT STREET

HILL SMITH GALLERY
(1864, 1910)

Under the house paint on the wall behind the fine art in Hill Smith Gallery is an advertisement for a large Kawasaki motorbike – invisible testimony to the versatility of many Adelaide buildings. Before the paintings, the gallery was a printing workshop and then a motorcycle dealership. Along with its near identical neighbour two doors down, the building appears to have been preserved by intent rather than accident. That the pair has been preserved at all is a contrast to the other side of Pirie Street. Behind is the original Adelaide brewery, with its cellar, tunnels and malt tower.

DUNCAN & CO. LTD., 107–109 Pirie Street, Motor Accessories, Spare Parts and Radio.

EWER, AULD & CO. LTD., 99a Pirie Street, Hardware and Crockery Merchants.

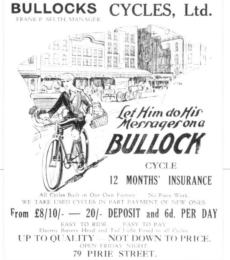

THE ALL-BRITISH MOTOR HOUSE LIMITED, 75 Pirie Street, South Australian distributors for Austin Cars. "You buy a car, but you invest in an Austin." Phone C. 8172.

BULLOCKS CYCLES LIMITED, 79 Pirie Street. Cycles built up to quality, not down to price. Save tram fares and buy a cycle. Twenty shillings deposit and sixpence a day. Phone C. 2618.

AUSTRALIAN GENERAL ELECTRIC LIMITED 73 Pirie St. Suppliers of: Mazda & Ediswan Lamps, Electric Accessories, Vacuum Cleaners and Washers, Refrigerators and Fans, Hotpoint Appliances, Motors, Generators, Switchgears. Phone C. 8210 (3 lines).

MAZDA HOUSE

A.V. COTTRELL, Tailor and Costumier, established 1908, is at 67 Pirie Street. He also specialises in cleaning and pressing.

At 63-65, Pirie Street, on the corner of Gawler Place, is the **ELLIOTT CYCLE STORES.** This is the home of the famous Super Elliott Cycles. All accessories are obtainable here. Catalogues free on application. Phone C. 236.

SALVATION ARMY PEOPLE'S PALACE

FREEMASONS HOTEL

PIRIE STREET (SOUTH SIDE), BETWEEN WYATT STREET AND GAWLER PLACE

Continuing renovations to the Salvation Army's landmark People's Palace for homeless men meant it wasn't photogenic enough for *Progressive Adelaide*. Now a facade, the French Renaissance-style Palace was first the German Club. Seven men died in a fire there in 1975, and the Salvos left the building four years later. The Freemasons Hotel next door got the art deco treatment while the All-British Motor House became the Planet nightclub of recent memory. Before that, Bullocks' advised, "Save tram fares and buy a cycle". Both conveyances are back in favour. The enigmatic little arts and craftsy Mazda House is almost intact. Not so the plain shops across the lane, but a well-detailed commercial building now defines the corner. On the street it is known, with respect, as "The Blue Loo".

Pirie Street, 1927 with the State Bank building in progress.

THE EPWORTH BOOK DEPOT, on the ground floor of the Epworth Building, is an up-to-date, and well-appointed Book and Stationery Shop. It is equipped with books to suit all tastes. Phone: C. 762.

INTERIOR VIEW OF THE JUVENILE AND S.S. DEPARTMENT
of the
EPWORTH BOOK DEPOT
EPWORTH BUILDING, PIRIE STREET

PIRIE STREET CHURCH

QUEEN'S CHAMBERS (1869)

GLADSTONE CHAMBERS (1880)

EAGLE CHAMBERS (1879)

GAWLER PLACE

KING WILLIAM STREET

PIRIE STREET (SOUTH SIDE), BETWEEN GAWLER PLACE AND KING WILLIAM STREET

FORMER STATE BANK OF SOUTH AUSTRALIA (1927)

EPWORTH BUILDING (1926)

COLONEL LIGHT CENTRE

Edmund Wright's Union Bank graced the Gawler Place corner for 77 years, shaded at first by eucalypts. It came down in the 1920s, as the original State Bank of South Australia went up. The bank was overlooked in *Progressive Adelaide*, but is likely soon to have a new life as a heritage facade for a 22-storey tower. The striking Gothic-style Epworth Building is a State Bank contemporary. Pirie Street Wesleyan Church was the spiritual focus of Methodism in South Australia, with the Epworth its commercial reach. The Epworth is untouchable, but the church failed to survive. It gave way to the Adelaide City Council's Colonel Light Centre administration building, although the Methodist Meeting Hall behind retains some 19th-century religious flavour. Little Queen's Chambers, with its cantilevered balcony and Italianate charm, is more a whisper than an echo of colonial days.

The "COMPLETE" Motor, Motorcycle, Cycle, Radio and Electrical Organisation

THE HEALING MACHINE AND ELECTRICAL SHOPS
IN HANSON STREET

SPARE PARTS
For all CARS, TRUCKS, AND TRACTORS

We carry a comprehensive range of spare parts, the majority of which are manufactured in the modern Healing factory, and backed with the Healing guarantee.

Every section of the Motor Trade is catered for and "Service" is our password.

IN THIS SECTION TRADE ONLY SUPPLIED

EVERYTHING ELECTRICAL

You are invited to inspect our modern electrical showrooms where the entire electrical trade is catered for.

We are South Australian Agents for:

The British General Electric Company Limited

Manufacturers of the Famous:

'Magnet' Electrical Appliances

The HEALING *Electric* REFRIGERATOR

is the Last Word in Modern Electric Refrigeration

Healing Refrigerators have been designed from a notable American model with full patent right. They have the advantage, therefore, of many years of research work, and incorporate America's last minute improvements. Additionally, there are features planned exclusively by Healing engineers. The Healing is a superior refrigerator in every way—silent, economical, reliable, and fast in freezing.

—EASY TERMS ARRANGED.

Modernize the Home and Office with Healing
STEEL TUBE FURNITURE
IT'S COMFORTABLE, STRONG, NEAT, AND HYGIENIC
Call and Let Us Show You Our Modern Range.

HEALING offers you

THE FINEST MACHINE SHOP SERVICE IN SOUTH AUSTRALIA

Specialists in Line Boring of Connecting Rods and Main Bearings.

Modern equipment and the latest methods are the keynote of Healing Machine Shop Services. There are facilities for handling all classes of work from reboring to armature rewinding and battery repairs. By using Healing's Machine Shop, you save your time, reduce your costs and increase your profits. Satisfaction is GUARANTEED.

Telephone: Central 4633 (7 lines)

We carry the most comprehensive range of cycle parts and accessories in the State, also everything for the motorcycle trade. TRADE ONLY.

There's a Healing Cycle for every purpose and to suit every pocket. Terms from 10/- deposit and 3/- weekly. A few agencies still available. Manufactured in the Healing factory which is the most up-to-date in the Commonwealth.

HEALING CYCLES FAMOUS IN QUALITY SINCE 1896

Recognised as the standard of High-class Radio.

Call and Inspect Our Huge Range of Radio Accessories at Remarkably Low Prices.

Section of a Large Crowd Assembled in Hindmarsh Square enjoying a Cricket Re-Diffusion which has been commented on as being the finest thing of its kind in the Commonwealth.

A. G. HEALING LIMITED

WAREHOUSE: 151-159 PIRIE STREET ———————— **MACHINE AND ELECTRICAL SHOPS: HANSON STREET, ADELAIDE**

ALSO SYDNEY, MELBOURNE, HAMILTON, HORSHAM, AND SALE

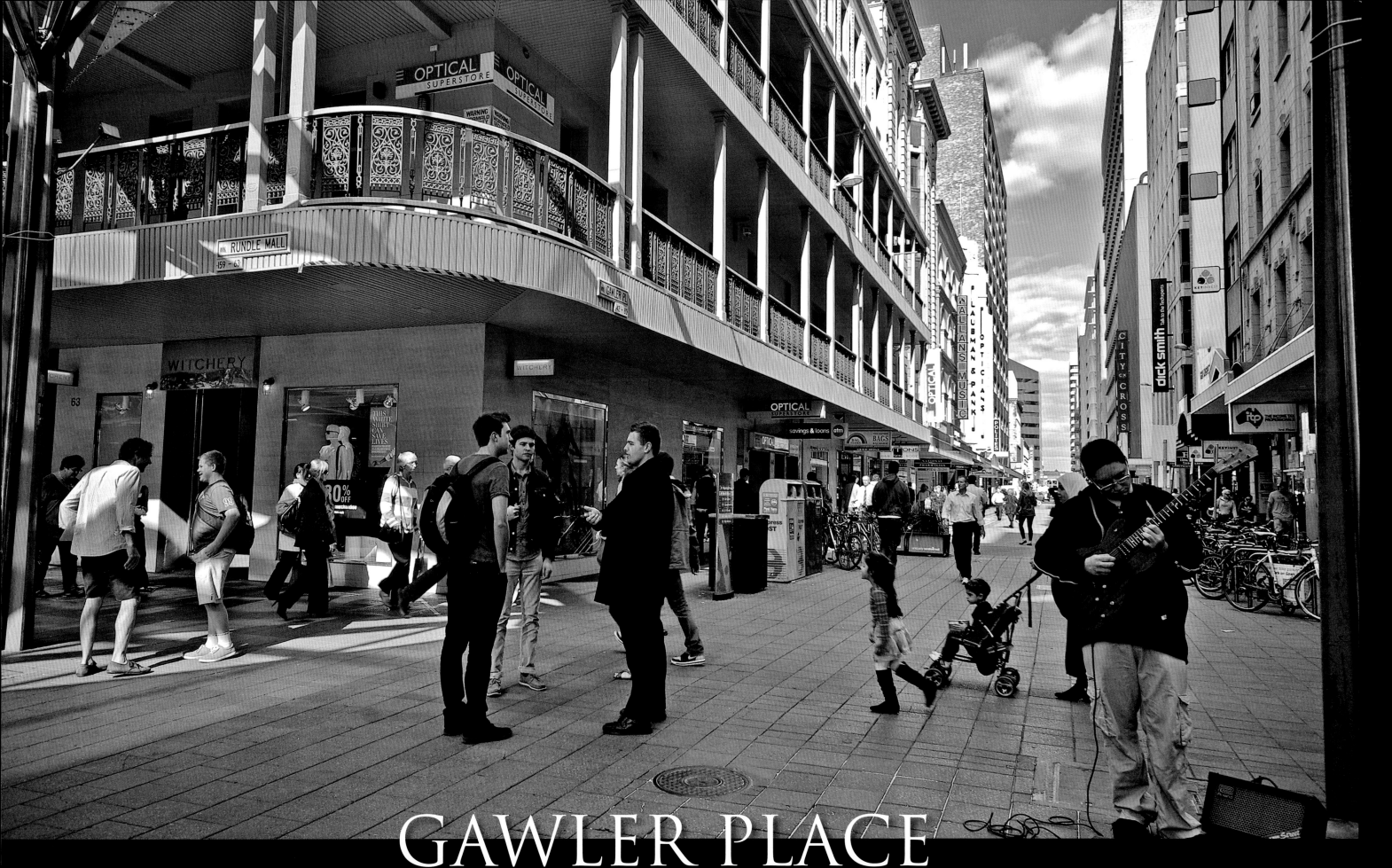

GAWLER PLACE

SUHARD & CO., 46 Gawler Place, Watchmakers, Gem and Diamond Ring Specialists. Phone: C. 2567. "MONTE" MILK BAR, 48 Gawler Place, is renowned for its high-class of genuine Fruit-Flavoured Malted Milk Drinks. The modern Toilet Salon of "GLORIETTE" (Mr. and Mrs. E. Sammons) 50 Gawler Place. This Salon has recently been modernised and brought into line with salons overseas. Mr. and Mrs. Sammons have completed a twelve-months' tour of England and the Continent, where they studied all the latest modes of hairdressing and permanent waving. Clients are assured of first class attention under the personal supervision of Mrs. Sammons. All towels, combs, instruments, etc., are thoroughly sterilized. Phone: C. 3511. CLARIDGE HOUSE AND ARCADE (1927) CLARIDGE HOUSE is a fine building, with an arcade, shops, offices and professional chambers. The Toilet Salon of MISS GENE HAINS, occupies the basement. This Salon is one of the largest and oldest-established beauty parlors in South Australia. The fine lounge, tastefully furnished, is the largest in the city. Twelve dainty cubicles and a staff of expert operators assure patrons of comfort and work of the highest class. Phone: C. 2525. LAMSON PARAGON LIMITED, Manufacturers of Sales Check Books, Multiple Copy Books and Forms. For handwriting the Paragon Register provides speed, security, and perfect copies. For typewriting, the Paragon Parafold and Parabar fit any typewriter and give speed, convenience and carbon handling. Phone: C. 4650. THE LAVENDER GARDEN, 1st floor, is the most exclusive tea rooms in Adelaide, and is one of the most expensively equipped places of its kind in the Commonwealth. Tables may be reserved. C. 4169. NELL HILL'S Modern Toilet Salon, 2nd floor. Permanent-Waving a speciality. Phone: C. 1201. MARIE DE VAL, 2nd Floor, Designer and Maker of exclusive models in Frocks, Costumes, etc. NANCY BEAUMONT 2nd Floor, caters for Hosiery Repairing, general mending & darning. Phone: C. 455. MISS W.D. GURNER, 3rd Floor, Dressmaker and Costumier. Phone: C. 4058. MISS M.D. SMITH, Hemstitching Expert, is on the 4th floor. All work receives personal, prompt attention. F.J.A. LORRAIN, 5th Floor. Jewellers, engravers. Inscriptions, Monograms, Family Crests, Brass and Silver Plates, Shields. Phone: C. 5949. LUCILE, Specialist in Children's Garments. Hand-made and Smocking are specialities. Phone: C. 2735. MISS G. ADLAM, Florist. Fresh Cut Flowers daily. Wedding Orders, Posies, Sheafs, & Wreaths on shortest notice. C. 5535. JIM McDOWALL LIMITED, the Intimate Sports Depot. Where advice and information are given free on all sports matters. Where each member of the staff is young, keen, and enthusiastic. THE STANDARD RUBBER CO. All latest methods of Birth Control. Only the highest-grade Contraceptive & Rubber Goods stocked. DAVEY & WARNER, Tailors and Costumiers. Phone: C. 2334. MISSES N. & M. WHILLAS, Art Needlework & Woolcraft Specialists. Tapestry Designs. College and Club Badges executed. Hemstitching executed at shortest notice. Phone: C. 1528. GRIFFITHS BROS

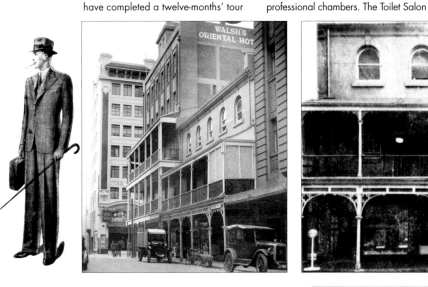

PHONE : C. 3988

G. Jamieson

LADIES' and
GENTS'
TAILOR

38. FOURTH FLOOR

CLARIDGE HOUSE

Gawler Place.

GAWLER PLACE (EAST SIDE), BETWEEN RUNDLE MALL AND GRENFELL STREET

NATIONAL PHARMACIES   ALLANS MUSIC

Woman of the arts Patricia Hackett, who threw ink at critics, ran her avant garde Torch Theatre in the basement of Claridge Arcade in Claridge House, now home to National Pharmacies. Much later, the basement became Big Daddy's, a lunchtime disco with go-go girls. Griffiths Bros once dispensed their teas, coffees and cocoas next to where Allans Music is today. Blue enamel signs along the rail and tram tracks would proclaim the number of "miles to Griffiths Bros teas". How these distances were calculated remains unclear, because trains or trams have never run along Gawler Place.

When requiring anything in Pictures, a visit to **J. HOOPER**, Art Dealer and Picture Framer, 64 Gawler Place, will convince you that the greatest value in the city is obtainable here. Hooper's are antique work specialists. Picture frames of all descriptions. Phone: C. 5926.

EKERS & ROBINSON, 64 Gawler Place. The "CORRECT TAILORING SERVICE." Known for 30 years for smart style and consistent value. Phone: C. 2692.

H.L. SAUNDERS AND P. HUNT, 68a Gawler Place, Gentlemen's High-Class Hairdressers and Tobacconists. Hygienic service. Expert attention. Six chairs.

GAWLER PLACE (EAST SIDE), BETWEEN RUNDLE MALL AND GRENFELL STREET

LAUBMAN & PANK BUILDING
(1863, 1934)

FORMER DA COSTA BUILDING (1957)

Retail business began on the ground floors, at the front doors, so that's where the camera turned for *Progressive Adelaide*. The narrow confines of Gawler Place allowed no alternative. The Laubman & Pank building, originally designed by no less than George Strickland Kingston as a bluestone warehouse, could not be captured in all its new art deco gear. Laubman & Pank, still a national name in eyewear, gave the former Colonial Architect's building its fresh start after the optical firm had grown from Adelaide to Australia-wide.

"If you want a suit that's becoming to you, you've got to be coming to me." **WORTHLEY'S**, Tailors, corner Gawler Place and Pirie Street. Phone: C. 5683.

Flowers are playing a great part in the Centenary Celebrations. All festivities are including floral displays. For Floral displays bearing that artistic Touch that is so desirable, **MABEL HARDINGE, ART FLORIST**, of 115 Gawler Place, is always pleased to advise and supply you. Fresh Cut Flowers, Choice of Posies, Bouquets, Wreaths, and Boxes of Flowers are always obtainable. Bridal Bouquets a speciality. Open Sunday mornings from 10 a.m. to 12. Phone: C. 8968. After hours, U 4896.

Since the days of Eve it has been said that "Woman's hair is her crowning glory." Hairdressing executed at the **"KARO" TOILET SALON**, 115 Gawler Place, assures this glory. Permanent Waves executed here have a distinctive appearance, and are easy to keep set. Marcel and Water-Waving, Tinting, Face and Scalp Massage and Treatments, and all classes of beauty culture are carried out by skilled operators. Phone: C. 8968.

LEWIS CYCLE WORKS LTD., 111 Gawler Place (also at Port Pirie). Manufacturers of Lewis High Grade CYCLES AND INVALID CHAIRS. Full stock of accessories. Phone: C. 1469.

J. MOODIE, Practical Watchmaker and Jeweller, 109 Gawler Place, Repairs a speciality. Old gold bought. Phone: C. 3858

Referring to your next Suit, **C.H. PHILLIPS**, of 3 McHenry Street (off Gawler Place), has the latest smart English and Australian Suitings at lowest prices that will more than compare with anything offered with Quality, Cut, Workmanship, and Prices are considered. Phone: C. 2962

BULLEN'S CINEMAS AND CAMERAS LTD., 105 Gawler Place. The home of new and second-hand Cameras, Home Cinemas, Standard Talkie Equipment, Films, Lanterns, Slide library, Commercial and Home Photography, Developing and Printing Service. Phone: C. 6971.

PIRIE STREET

McHENRY STREET

GAWLER PLACE (WEST SIDE), BETWEEN PIRIE STREET AND GRENFELL STREET

Gawler Place got the better of Baring. It was like taking pictures in a cupboard, so he settled in the end for a typeset GAWLER PLACE DIRECTORY which promised that you could learn the latest American tap dancing routine in 10 lessons by day, then go out and conquer Adelaide by night. What Baring did capture of this precinct's Victorian bluestone though, is now all gone.

J.T. STEVENS' Sports Depot is at 101 Gawler Place. Same-Day Repair Service. C. 2228.

THE COMMERCIAL HOTEL (T. Woodhead), 95 Gawler Place. Accommodation for visitors. Phone: C. 2228.

HUGH POZZA, Parisian Tailor, 91 Gawler Place. Latest from the Continent and America. Established in Adelaide since 1928.

L.P. DEAN, Practical Watchmaker and Jeweller, at 89 Gawler Place, specialises in watches of all descriptions. Christmas and Centenary Presents on view.
FORD BROS DRY CLEANERS AND DYERS Gawler Place. C. 3838.

GEO. R. WILLIAMS, High-Class Gentlemen's Hairdresser and Tobacconist, is at 85 Gawler Place.

GRENFELL STREET

GAWLER PLACE (WEST SIDE), BETWEEN PIRIE STREET AND GRENFELL STREET

He was in time to record Vitrolite, the wonder material of the 1920s. The low-maintenance coloured glass was in demand for theatres and cinemas, and simple shop fronts like Ford Bros Dry Cleaners and Dyers. It came in black, orange and sanitary green, and fitted easily with art deco and art nouveau.

HUGHES-ADAMS LTD.
(Principals of which are C.J. HUGHES, late of T. and G. Building, and R.B. ADAMS, late of Compton Adams, Ltd., Grenfell Street), Tailors, 73 Gawler Place. Tailoring confined to genuine bespoke work at prices within the range of the average wage-earner. Up-to-date styles are specially featured. Phone: C. 8563.

A.A. GWYNNE, Gentlemen's Hairdresser and Tobacconist, is situated at 75 Gawler Place.

F. FILMER (FILMER AND AMOORE), 67 Gawler Place. "The Quality Shoe Store." Phone: C. 6311.

Y.M.C.A.   **WOMEN'S WORK DEPOT**

GAWLER PLACE (WEST SIDE), BETWEEN GRENFELL STREET AND RUNDLE MALL

CITY CROSS

Before the arrival of the shopping mall, traditional "high street" strip shopping created living street scenes. This part of Gawler Place had the usual hairdresser, tobacconist, watchmaker, shoe shop, a branch of the YMCA and the Women's Work Depot. The WWD's purpose was "to help women earn a partial livelihood by the sale of any hand-made goods". Mending of all kinds was undertaken, not least "invisible darning of ladders in stockings". In the 21st century the shopping mall, like City Cross here, hides valuable customer services such as invisible darning by internalising all the action.

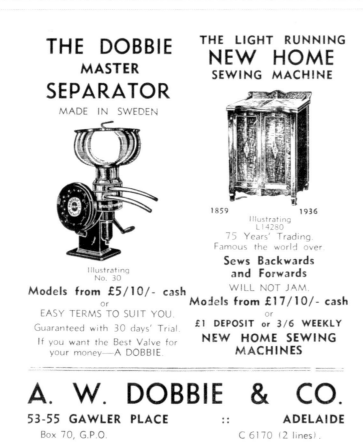

GAWLER PLACE (WEST SIDE), BETWEEN GRENFELL STREET AND RUNDLE MALL

PHARMACY BUILDING (1925)

Carrangis' Fish, Oyster and Grill Saloon was the old way of lunching for city workers and shoppers – table service and orders cooked while you waited. Today, City Cross has a busy, large international food court – instant service for those who eat and run. Alexander Dobbie, who gave his name to the long-gone shopfront here, was a fair dinkum colonial character. A foundry owner, travel writer, serial inventor and Sunday School teacher, he designed an electric writing pen. Dobbie was fascinated by hypnosis for the relief of dental pain, mesmerism and clairvoyance. He was believed to be the first person in the Southern Hemisphere to make a telephone, which he put in his greenhouse in College Park. In his time Alexander Dobbie was an Adelaide tourist attraction, a local rock star of The Age of Inventions.

Keep the Children's Playground Clean with *Electrolux*

the only Cleaning System that does all these things for you

More than 100,000 Australian housewives have abandoned the unhealthy and tiring labour of brooms, dust-distributing carpet sweepers, and back-breaking "hands-and-knees" polishing . . . Why? Because Electrolux is the only cleaning method to do every job easily, quickly, and thoroughly! And remember, Electrolux is the most economical cleaner to buy and use. Write to-day for a demonstration in your own home, by our Newcastle Representative without obligation.

① Gives you a complete home-cleaning service by which carpets, stairs, upholstery, curtains, etc., can be thoroughly cleaned with rapidity and ease.

② Cleans and polishes linoleums and bare floors with one quick, easy operation.

③ Destroys moths and silverfish in carpets, upholstery, clothes, etc.

④ Purifies the air of dust and germs.

⑤ Sprays insecticide, disinfectant, or paint.

⑥ Grooms dogs, cats, horses, etc.

⑦ Shampoos and airs carpets.

⑧ Gives noiseless operation.

⑨ Operates as a hair drier.

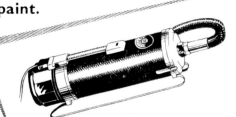

ELECTROLUX   THE MODERN HOME CLEANER

Head Office - - - - - - - 415 BOURKE STREET, MELBOURNE, C.1.

Branch Office - - - - - - - - 120 RUNDLE STREET, ADELAIDE

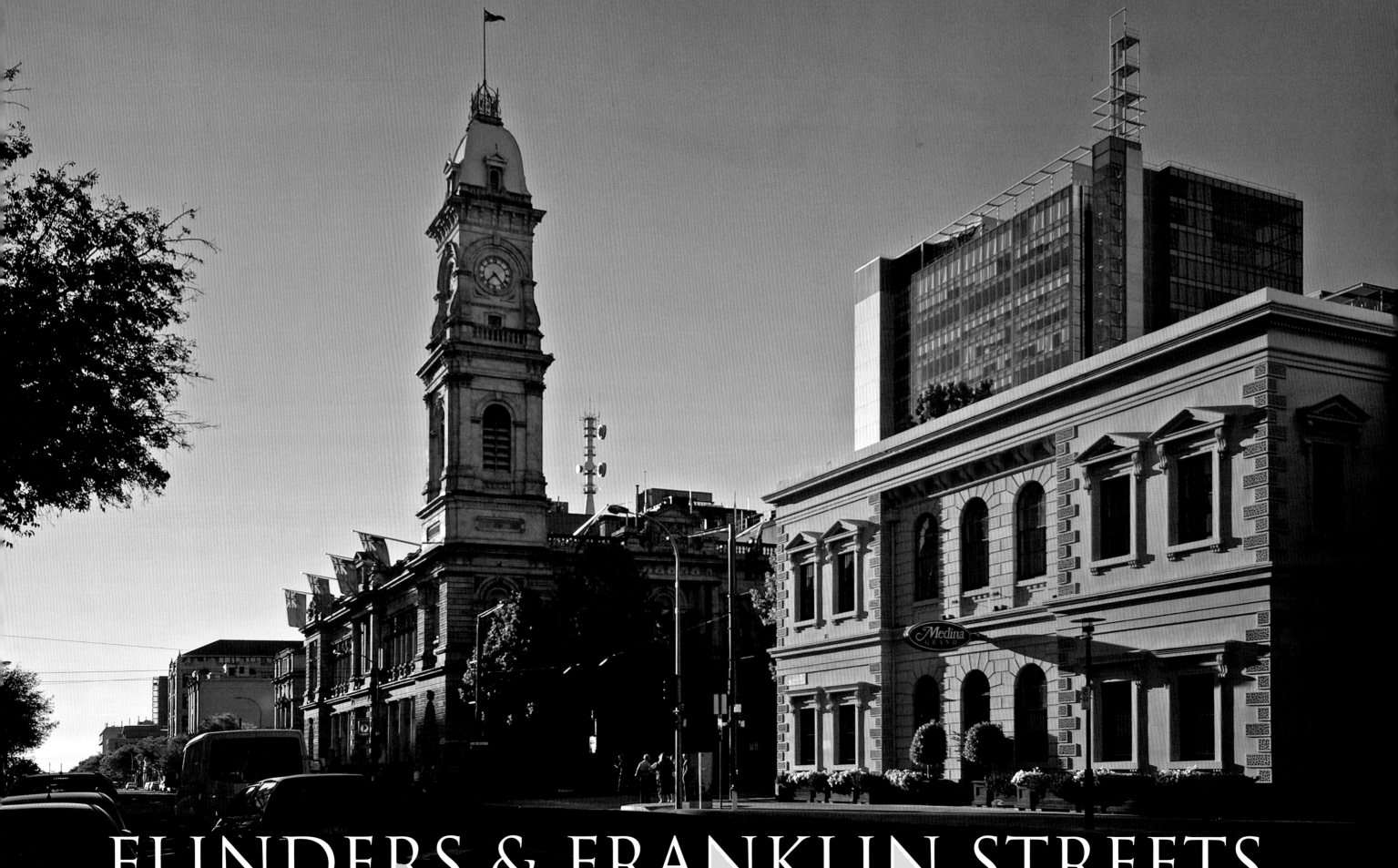

FLINDERS & FRANKLIN STREETS

GOVERNMENT OFFICES/TREASURY BUILDINGS (1839–1874)

STOW MEMORIAL CHURCH AND MANSE in 1873.

KING WILLIAM STREET

VICTORIA PLACE

FLINDERS STREET (NORTH SIDE), BETWEEN KING WILLIAM STREET AND VICTORIA PLACE

PILGRIM CHURCH

MULTICULTURAL AFFAIRS SA

The Government Offices, or Treasury Buildings, remain essentially unchanged since the 19th century, despite their present vocation as a luxury hotel. Similarly, the squirrel in the middle front pillar of Pilgrim Church has been there since 1867, when the Congregational flock built the place of worship as a memorial to the pioneering Reverend T.Q. Stow. Next door the manse was completed two years later. Early in the next century the manse became Dr Hynes' sanatorium after its excellent conversion from Gothic to Classic. The doctor believed people got better in happy surroundings, so he would often pack his patients off to a concert or the theatre. The old manse/sanatorium is now home to Multicultural Affairs SA, but a 27-level hotel/office tower behind the manse is on the cards. The manse should become a heritage hotel, like the Treasury.

CHROMIUM PLATING ...
MOTOR CAR AND CYCLE WORK
A SPECIALITY
SILVERPLATING OF TABLEWARE AND
BRASS BAND INSTRUMENTS

B. WALLIS & CO.
52 FLINDERS STREET, ADELAIDE

B. WALLIS & CO., established 45 years, 52 Flinders St. Electroplaters, Chromium Platers. Will replate anything, including cutlery and all table-ware equal to new. Motor car chromium plating a speciality. Brass band instruments silver plated. Phone C. 5517.

FLINDERS STREET (NORTH SIDE), BETWEEN VICTORIA PLACE AND FREEMASONS LANE

SANTOS CENTRE

B. Wallis & Co., just left of today's Santos Centre, were electroplaters and chromium platers. They would "replate anything", including silver-plating brass band instruments. In South Australia's centenary year, with music in the air from street parades and rotunda concerts, brass bands everywhere, B. Wallis & Co. could expect a huge demand for electroplating. The Santos Centre has a gently tapering pop out window from the fifth level to the top. This means that if you sit in the two suspended chairs to the upper left of the building in this photo, you experience the sensation of swinging in space.

LENSWORTH HOUSE
(1925)

OBSERVATORY HOUSE
(1906)

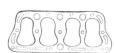

FLINDERS STREET (NORTH SIDE), BETWEEN FREEMASONS LANE AND HYDE STREET

The tower of Observatory House symbolises seeing clearly. Underneath it, optician George Kohler made spectacles, lorgnettes, binoculars and telescopes. He bought the business from scientific instrument maker Otto Boettger, who invented a machine for heating and cooling drinks that would prove an instant hit in the hospitality world. Later George built the interwar Lensworth House office block directly west, and moved his factory in. Upon rising each morning, he continued to see clearly from his Observatory House tower.

FLINDERS STREET (NORTH SIDE), BETWEEN HYDE STREET AND PULTENEY STREET

Adelaide took eclectic architecture to its heart in the State's centenary year. It could boast a wide variety of styles for a wide variety of uses, as this often-overlooked street frontage demonstrates. Today the view is much more conformist – all the small titles have been consolidated west of Hanson Street, now Pulteney. The big buildings on both sides down this end look nothing like old Flinders Street, but they are not ashamed to be modernist.

The Adelaide Fire Brigade fights the fire at Dunlop Perdriau Rubber Company.

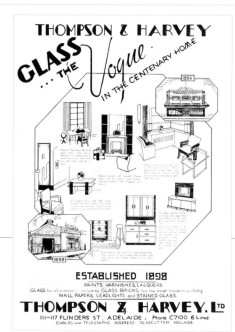

FLINDERS STREET (SOUTH SIDE), BETWEEN PULTENEY STREET AND DIVETT PLACE

Resembling a giant stack of crumpled cardboard, a "leaning tower of Adelaide" residential development is proposed for the vacant block at left. Seventy-odd years ago Miss Campbell of the London Hotel must have longed for a quieter life. The Thompson & Harvey paint store directly east of her was rebuilt after a fire. Soon the fire engines were back on the other side of her establishment, at Dunlop Perdriau, fighting a rubber conflagration that plumed black smoke as far away as Unley. The latter fire victim has survived after a fashion, the former has gone to Telstra. Miss Campbell is nowhere to be seen. Unlike other denominations, the Baptists have kept most of their churches over the past 150 years, which is why the Gothic revival Flinders Street church is such a sanctuary in the city. Modern plate doors have been added, very sensibly, to keep out the street noise.

FLINDERS STREET
BAPTIST CHURCH
(1861–1863)

LIVERPOOL BUILDING
(1925)

A.N.A BUILDING (1928)
AUSTRALIAN NATIVES'
ASSOCIATION. The National
Benefit Society. Built by
Australians for Australians.
Founded to protect the interests
of Australia as a Nation.
Branches throughout all States.
ANDREW M. RANKINE, Room
16, second floor. Gentlemen's
Tailor and Ladies' Costumier.
Phone: U 2455. **T.M. POLLOCK**,
Medical Gymnast, Masseur,

Room 31, third floor. **"LA**
AISNE" School of Dresscutting,
Designing and Making.
Third floor. **FRANK CORK**,
Commercial Artist, No. 11,
Second Floor. Phone: C. 1560.
LORNA M. WOOLCOCK,
Hand-Painted China Gifts
& Souvenirs. Commercial
Art Studio 3rd Floor. **W.T.**
CLIFFORD, Hairdresser and
Tobacconist is in this building.
All smokers' requisites.

EDUCATION BUILDING

MOTOR VEHICLES DEPARTMENT

GAWLER PLACE

VICTORIA SQUARE

FLINDERS STREET (SOUTH SIDE), BETWEEN DIVETT PLACE AND VICTORIA SQUARE

FORMER RESERVE BANK BUILDING (1968)

The former Liverpool and Australian Natives' Association buildings make a good couple, not much changed throughout their lifetimes. The ANA was built "by Australians for Australians. Founded to protect the interests of Australia as a Nation". Across Gawler Place, the National Trust didn't consider the Edwardian Baroque Education Building worth saving. Neither did the State Government, which sent in the bulldozers. Soon the same fate befell the Grand Central Hotel at Rundle and Pulteney, and Adelaide had lost its two fine Mayfair-style buildings that possessed genuine grandeur. Imagine them as five-star hotels today, this one close to a rethought Victoria Square and the Market. The government said the Education Building's "accommodation" wasn't up to scratch, for which read mainly "air conditioning". The bush-hammered pre-cast concrete replacement has sun shading and is cool in summer. The flat, squat section appears an under-performing asset that could go skywards for affordable housing. Once symbolic of prestige, wealth and the security of our monetary system, the institutional architecture Reserve Bank building of 1968 is offices now. But what a place to live on Victoria Square!

◄ **DUNCAN BUILDING** The fine **DUNCAN BUILDING** at 42–54 Franklin Street is now divided into motor showrooms on the ground floor and offices, professional chambers, up above. The up-to-date and spacious showrooms of **SPORTING CARS LTD.**, sole distributors of Packard, Auburn, and Riley cars, are on the ground floor, western section. This is the home of the New Packard, 120 Series. The modern showrooms of **LYNAS AND FENWICK LTD.**, Sole Distributors for Hupmobile and Rover cars, are on the eastern section of the ground floor. The Service Station and Used Car Departments are also housed in this establishment.
DUNCAN AGENCIES Manufacturers' Agents. Manufacturers! We are calling regularly on all chemists, stores, grocers, beauty parlors, etc., throughout the State, and can give individual and enthusiastic attention to manufacturers desiring live representation. First Floor. Phone: C. 6002. **A. LYALL LUSH**, first floor, for Commercial Art and Design. Phone: C. 6000.
TUCKER'S USED CARS, the Leading House for good class cars and trucks, where you get an honest deal, a good allowance for your present car, reasonable terms, and reliable service. Call and see Tucker's large range, all popular makes, and at prices to suit all buyers. Second Floor. Phone: C. 3000.

FRANKLIN STREET (NORTH SIDE), BETWEEN YOUNG STREET AND KING WILLIAM STREET

◄ Where the Adelaide 36ers began: the State's first basketball association formed in the centenary year, when all games were played in the car showrooms of the Duncan Building. The Duncan car body company was hard hit by the full importation of Fords, then the Depression. In 1936, the Duncans were desperate to sell their building, and *Progressive Adelaide* gave them two pages to do it. "Can you visualise the increment in values as the years pass? It is impossible to foretell . . ." ran the ad. Eventually the Postmaster-General moved his telephone exchange in there. Latest plans are for a multi-million dollar glass office tower and car park. The Duncan family could not have foretold that.

HENRY BERRY & CO. PTY LTD., Proprietors "Invicta" Groceries, Wholesale Grocers and General Merchants. Suppliers of – Bakers, Butchers, Confectioners' Requisites, Refrigerators, Scales, Cash Registers and all Shop Equipment. Phone: C. 3126. **WALTER AND MORRIS LTD.**, Timber Merchants, Franklin Street (Head Office) and Mills, Dale Street, Port Adelaide. Many years' experience in buying and milling timber enables this company to give customers the best value procurable. Established 1865.

FRANKLIN STREET (SOUTH SIDE), BETWEEN VICTORIA SQUARE AND TRADES HALL LANE

The cream-tiled little old Bank of Adelaide on the Morialta Street corner, now rebadged, is one of the city's cutest art deco changeups. Its bijou charms are hard to resist. People stop and smile. After 55 years as city base for the McBride pastoral empire, the equally charming Faraway House is now home to residential land developer Burke Urban, who gave it a facelift in 2009. McBrides set up another Faraway House at Wayville, near the Showground. Everybody's happy.

FARAWAY HOUSE

T. COLLINS, Gentlemen's Hairdresser and Tobacconist, at 35 Franklin Street, is always pleased to see you. Cleanliness and good workmanship always.

ADELAIDE MOTOR WRECKING CO. LTD., Wreckers of all makes of cars and trucks. New and Secondhand Parts, Tyres, Tubes, Radiators, Generators, Magnetos, etc. New Batteries (rubber-cased), 25/-. Rear Luggage Carriers, 12/6. 37 Franklin Street Phone: C. 5567. **A. SENN**, 37 Franklin Street, Auto-Electrical Repairs. Battery Re-Charging and Repairs.

ROY MORRIS, Adelaide's leading Tailor and Mercer—established 17 years—is on the corner of Pitt Street. A State-wide reputation assures you of fit, style, workmanship and complete satisfaction. Phone: C. 4252.

PITT STREET:

R.G. BAYLY, 11 Pitt Street, Duco Enameller and Motor Trimmer, will brighten up your car with Duco at a reasonable price. Phone: C. 6800.

F.A. CANN, 4–6 Pitt Street, Draper. Specialist in Ladies' Wear and Manchester Goods.

FRANKLIN STREET (SOUTH SIDE), BETWEEN TRADES HALL LANE AND PITT STREET

After World War II, Great Britain rebuilt many of its bombed-out churches along highly geometric lines. Maughan Uniting Church here fits this description, almost Gaudi-like in its present manifestation. The church's social history is strong, and the Sunday afternoon sermon often made news. Steps, and then an aluminium ladder, led to the very top of the tower, not an ascent for those of little faith. If you are slightly disoriented here, the first church was in behind Roy Morris the tailor, but facing Franklin Street.

MAUGHAN UNITING CHURCH

**PHIL O'NEILL'S CAR
EXCHANGE**, The Truck King.
63 Franklin Street. Specialists
in used cars and trucks. See
us for a fair deal. Phones: C.
6466, after hours: L 5477.
DINGLE MOTOR CO.,
specialists in all classes of
Automobile Repairs. Metal
workers.

DOMINION MOTORS LTD., 81
Franklin Street, Sales and Service
for the popular 'English Standard'
cars throughout South Australia
and Broken Hill. "The English car
whose sales are increasing faster
than any other." A fine range of
quality used cars always in stock.
Phone: C. 2136.

DALGETY'S MOTORS (1924)

FRANKLIN STREET (SOUTH SIDE), BETWEEN PITT STREET AND BOWEN STREET

ADELAIDE CENTRAL BUS STATION

Half a century ago the city went mad for car parks and road widening. Now the sensible world is trying to reverse that trend. But if we must have car parks such as this one over the shops on the Pitt Street corner, it's better now that they are set back, with flats and offices hiding their true intent. The Dalgety's Motors building has lasted, although its core business is a pale shadow of yesteryear. Again, the argument goes that a facade is better than nothing, so there's room for a useful building behind. The new, airport-style Adelaide Central Bus Station has low-cost housing and a solar energy farm on the roof. It was the first stage in the continuing revival of the city's central west precinct, which fell just outside Baring's camera range.

GROTE STREET

◄ TIVOLI THEATRE, 1927

DREYER'S METROPOLITAN HOTEL, Two minutes from Post Office. Moderate Tariff. Adelaide's Leading Bottle Department, excellent accommodation, Hot water service. Phone: L 9271.

TUNNEY'S (1923)

JACK MEYER, the City's Leading Tailor, is at 34a Grote St. Eight hundred citizens are availing themselves of Jack Meyer's Suit Clubs; subscriptions, 2/6 weekly, and taking out a suit which is faultlessly tailored and which embodies the latest of fashions. Phone: C. 2322.

ALL CARS LTD. dealers in New and Used Cars, are at 28 Grote Street. Also authorised dealers of the New Willys "77." A demonstration can be arranged at any time. Repairs to all makes of cars by expert mechanics. Phone: C. 2229.

SARNIA BUILDING
CLARKE'S BIRD SHOP
COCKING'S FISH SHOP
METROPOLITAN GARAGE
& PARKING STATION

B.H. LEWIS, 22 Grote Street, High-Class Tailor and Costumier, who gives you the genuine hand-made article. Phone: C. 3576.

INDEPENDENT ORDER OF RECHABITES, SOUTH AUSTRALIAN DISTRICT NO. 81 The oldest, largest, and wealthiest Friendly Temperance Society. Branches in suburbs and most country towns. We are here to stay! Phone: C. 740.

PITT STREET · PENALUNA PLACE · TRADES HALL LANE · MORIALTA STREET

GROTE STREET (NORTH SIDE), BETWEEN PITT STREET AND MORIALTA STREET

METROPOLITAN HOTEL (1883)   **LA BOHEME**

The Princess, the Tivoli, His Majesty's, Her Majesty's again. South Australia's stage for all seasons has its own centenary in 2013. Only two letters in the name need to change for the next monarch. Top of the bill on opening night in 1913 was Lillie Langtry. But she wasn't the famous "Jersey Lilly" of the same name, King Edward VII's mistress. She was a music hall star, a Lillie Langtry impersonator, so we now know that Elvis didn't create the demand on his own. Right across from the Tivoli's stage door, the Metropolitan was Adelaide's 20th century showbiz hotel. Tunney's was the tobacco merchant for the generations, side by side with Jack Meyer, "the City's Leading Tailor", each suit "supervised by he himself". A half verandah post from the building's original treatment remains. Tunney's has become La Boheme, a popular cocktail and cabaret nightspot for young and emerging local performers. Sad that the Rechabites' two fine Italianate buildings don't remain too. They were dedicated to making "boys, girls, men and women, happy, sober and thrifty", not far down Grote Street from the music hall and the pub.

VICTORIA SQUARE

MARKET STREET

GROTE STREET (SOUTH SIDE), BETWEEN VICTORIA SQUARE AND MARKET CAR PARK

CENTRAL MARKET (1906)

Half of the 1906 red brick Federal Hall shops were bowled over for a new supermarket and arcade in the late 1960s. It had been a place for dances and wedding parties upstairs. Luckily for the Central Market most of the rest survived, for a time as a billiards hall. It's where the parking inspectors go for morning tea. Englishman George Grote, after whom this street is named, was friend and confidante to Robert Gouger, the first Colonial Secretary. He is better known for his 12-volume history of Greece. Nice one George, with Greek Australians for so many years the main ingredient in the multicultural mix that is the Central Market, between Grote and Gouger streets.

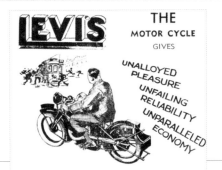
EMPIRE THEATRE

E.T. FISHER & CO. LTD., 65 Grote Street, Motor Cycle Importers and Dealers. Representing Norton, Levis, Coventry Eagle, Montgomery, and O.K. Supreme Motor Cycles. Phone: C. 1820.

LES. E. NORMAN, Motor Engineer, 69 Grote Street, repairs all makes of cars.

THE WEST ADELAIDE BOOK STORE (Miss M.T. Longbottom), 77 Grote Street. Periodicals on all subjects stocked or obtained to order. Country orders receive personal attention. Latest technical books stocked.

Your Petrol and Oil Requirements supplies at lowest prices at **HUBBARD MOTORS LTD.**, 85-87 Grote Street. Everything for Motor, Motorcycle, and Cycle. Look for the Gold and Blue Petrol Pump. The Confectionery, Cool Drink, and Refreshment Shop on the corner of Grote Street and West Side Central Market is now under the management of

Mrs. Nielsen, specialises in chocolate-dipped ice blocks. All flavours of milk and syrup blocks. All milk drinks, aerated drinks, hot or icy cold, are always available. **WILSON'S CAFE**, 91 Grote Street, cheapest and best Refreshments in Adelaide. Tea, one penny per cup. Centenary visitors, come here and save money.

CALIFORNIA STREET NORTH

MOONTA STREET

GROTE STREET (SOUTH SIDE), BETWEEN MARKET STREET AND MOONTA CAR PARK

MARKET PLAZA

CHINATOWN

In 1936 the new Empire Theatre offered "Three and a Half Hours of Solid Entertainment" at popular prices. Audience participation came naturally, because fruit from the market was always cheap. So the pianist for the silent movies played inside a wire cage. The fruit ran out for the Empire "bughouse" in 1952. These days its cast iron decorative verandah is the entrance to Market Plaza and on to Chinatown.

New Empire Theatre

61 Grote Street, New Adelaide

Three and a Half Hours of Solid Entertainment

POPULAR PRICES

WEDNESDAY NIGHTS—10d. PLUS TAX TO ALL PARTS

SATURDAY NIGHTS AND HOLIDAYS

STALLS—10d.   DRESS CIRCLE—1/-   (Plus Tax)

— Special Matinee for Children Saturday Afternoons —

"Well, What Did I Tell You!"

Overheard in the Crowd.

It was interval at a certain theatre. Crowds of people of all ages jostled their way through doors out into the vestibule; some to seek refreshment, others to smoke and yarn with friends. The writer happened to pause near a group of young men. With a knowing grin one turned to another and said: "Well, what did I tell you?"

Now, that's a remark which usually prefaces an argument, but the man at whom the query was levelled smiled back, and replied: "You're right, Jack. Guess I've been a darned fool, paying high admission money for talkie entertainment when I can secure dress circle seats at 1/2 and stall seats at 1/-, and, further, there is no tax to pay. If my young lady enjoys the rest of the programme we'll join the permanent patronage."

And, as he was well in evidence the following week, it is safe to presume that another man learnt sense. That theatre is the New Empire Theatre, Grote Street, New Adelaide, where 3½ hours of first-class talkie entertainment can be enjoyed at the cheapest admission charges in Adelaide.

Better Value.

The New Empire Theatre throws its doors open every Saturday afternoon and Saturday evening, and offers better value than any other theatre in the State, because every outstanding picture is shown. Do you know of any picture that has not been screened at the New Empire? If so, let the management know, and, if worth while, they will screen it. The management always strives after perfection by constantly studying the tastes and trend of permanent and prospective patrons.

Courteous Attention.

The New Empire Theatre, Grote Street, has all the latest appliances for providing the best entertainment of modern talkie houses. Besides, the new Empire is up-to-date, cool, and hygienic. The moment you say, "Two please," you become our guest, and the whole staff stands ready to render every desirable service. If you haven't already done so, make the New Empire Theatre your rendezvous—every Saturday and Wednesday.

FORMER MODEL SCHOOL (1874)

GROTE STREET (SOUTH SIDE), BETWEEN MOONTA STREET AND MORPHETT STREET

FORMER ADELAIDE HIGH SCHOOL

More than a century ago, Adelaide High School was the first non-private high school in the State. The boys later moved to a new state-of-the-art school in the West Park Lands, followed by the girls. Both sites are on the heritage list. The Grote Street buildings have since been home to an arts academy, wine centre and child care centre. They are generally well-preserved, as they should be. The sculptor John Dowie went here, as did the atomic physicist Mark Oliphant, a Governor of South Australia. Oliphant, sculpted by Dowie, is on North Terrace.

Moonta Street, a name that recalls an early mining boom, is at the heart of Adelaide's Chinatown. Every day is a dining boom.

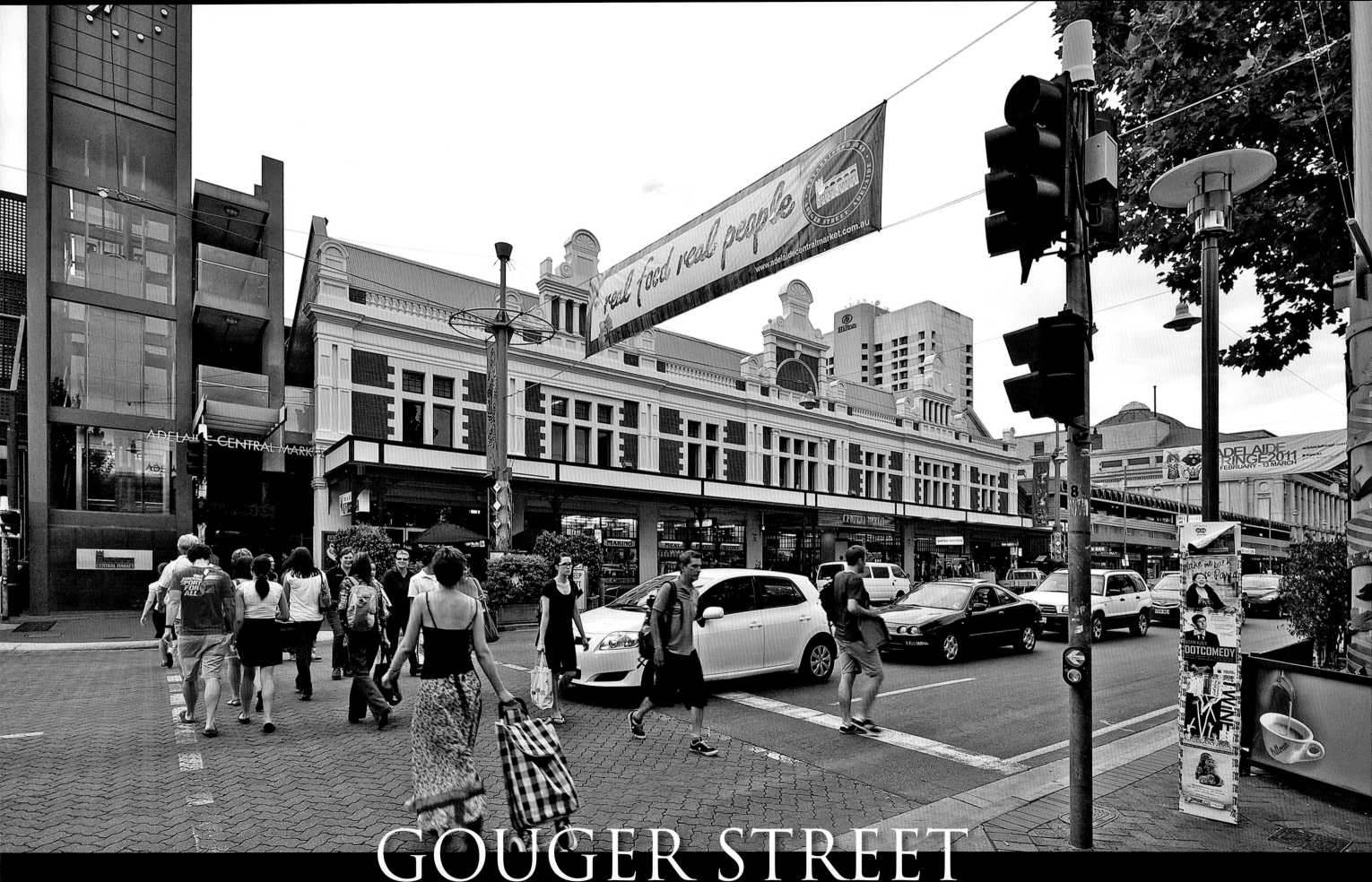

GOUGER STREET

S.O. BEILBY, Shipping and Retail Grocer and Provision Merchant, 62 Gouger Street.

BLACKS LIMITED, Boots, Shoes, Slippers, Hatters, Clothiers, Mercers.

CENTRAL MARKET
B. GOULD, 46–47 Central Market, for Men's Clothing, Manchester, Travelling Rugs, and Cases. **S. WILLAN**, 52 Central Market. Gent's Hairdresser & Tobacconist.

Razors ground and set.
SOUTH'S CAFE, 48–49 Central Market, caters for Light Luncheons, Afternoon Teas, etc. Rolls, Sandwiches, Cakes, etc.
A. JAMES has given twenty

GOUGER STREET (NORTH SIDE), BETWEEN CALIFORNIA STREET SOUTH AND MARKET STREET

MARKET PLAZA

With raw floorboards and no frills, Peoplestores was the store for everybody. In the fashion craze of the centenary decade, Peoplestores went from standard commercial to art deco in a year. In its heyday the store was so popular that the owners could buy the Empire Theatre and extend all the way to Grote Street. Now it is the Market Plaza with car park on the roof. Peoplestores is still remembered fondly.

years of reliable service at 56 Central Market. All classes of General Drapery, Mercery, and Clothing Manufactured. **W.J. HARRY**, 73 West Side Late Manager Tailoring and Men's Clothing Dept. with Peoplestores Limited), specialist in Men's Tailoring from three guineas. Country clients specially catered for. Phone: C. 4059. **THE FAIR DEAL STORES**, 72 Central Market, Drapery and Manchester Specialists. **ECONOMIC MEN'S STORES**, 59 Central Market, West Side. The working man's friend. Tailors, Outfitters, and Mercers. **CENTRAL** **PROVISION STORES**, Central Market, High Class Grocers, Provision and Tea Merchants. Phone: C. 126 (3lines).

CENTRAL MARKET ENTRANCE
(1906)

The 1906 two-storey southern entry to the Central Market is in the red brick and cream "blood and bandages" style. In 1936 Blacks Limited menswear made it a fashion statement in more ways than one. Now the former Blacks building is the main street statement of one of the best inner urban produce markets in the world. At one time the area even cultivated its own name, New Adelaide, and published its own newspaper – the New Adelaide News.

MOORE'S DEPARTMENT STORE

SUPREME COURT HOTEL (1885)

MILLS STREET

GOUGER STREET (NORTH SIDE) BETWEEN VICTORIA SQUARE AND MILL STREET

SIR SAMUEL WAY BUILDING

JEFFCOTT CHAMBERS

Not even the great fire of 1948 could drive away the Parisian charm of Moore's department store. The facade and grand staircase resisted the flames. In Moore's heyday, Father Christmas would arrive at its rooftop garden by aeroplane to the cheers of a thronged Victoria Square. When sales ceased, Moore's became the Sir Samuel Way Building, where justice is dispensed. The lawyers liked the Supreme Court Hotel so much that they bought it, then named it Jeffcott Chambers after South Australia's first judge Sir John Jeffcott, a successful duellist and Chief Justice of Sierra Leone. Its classic lines set the tone further down Adelaide's lawyers, eats and coffees street.

A.E. EWAN (GARD BROS.) Cycle &
Motor Works for New Cycles & Motors.
Repairs to all Makes of Cycles and
Motors. Showroom 21 Gouger Street
Phone: Central 659

COGLIN STREET

MARKET STREET

GOUGER STREET (SOUTH SIDE), BETWEEN MILL STREET AND MARKET STREET

Over the years as bike shops, banks, a hardware store, a post office, a shoe store and a tobacconist closed their doors, in their place restaurants, bars, coffee shops, cafes and
pizza joints have opened them again. The clutch of restaurants with the pagoda was once a carpet salesroom.

N. SOLOMON & CO. LTD.
Complete House Furnishers

Imperial lions guard Chinatown, and paper dragons dance in it. But Chinatown's sphere of influence widens far beyond its *paifangs*, or archways.

GOUGER STREET (SOUTH SIDE), BETWEEN MARKET STREET AND FIELD STREET

PAUL'S ON GOUGER

Adelaide's premier urban food precinct embraces Gouger and Grote streets, and is on course for Victoria Square. Paul's on Gouger restaurant set the modern precedent long ago. It moved into the laundry in Baring's photo in 1946 – not a bad innings for a fish and chip shop. Edson Arantes do Nascimento, also known as Pele, the world's greatest footballer, ate King George whiting there. In the time of fish-only on Fridays, there were queues at Paul's and Gouger Street's other great fish restaurants.

GOUGER STREET (SOUTH SIDE), BETWEEN FIELD STREET AND MORPHETT STREET

GAUCHO'S RESTAURANT

Gaucho's Restaurant, its Italianate style with added verandah, balcony and umbrellas to suit local conditions, was once a bicycle shop where wheelchairs were made. Even in the 1950s, Gouger Street's food rating was high: the Tuckerbox made one of Australia's first and best hamburgers, while the Lillydale Snack Bar's pineapple crush, dispensed next door to the bank that became a pizza joint and then the Star of Siam restaurant, won teenage hearts.

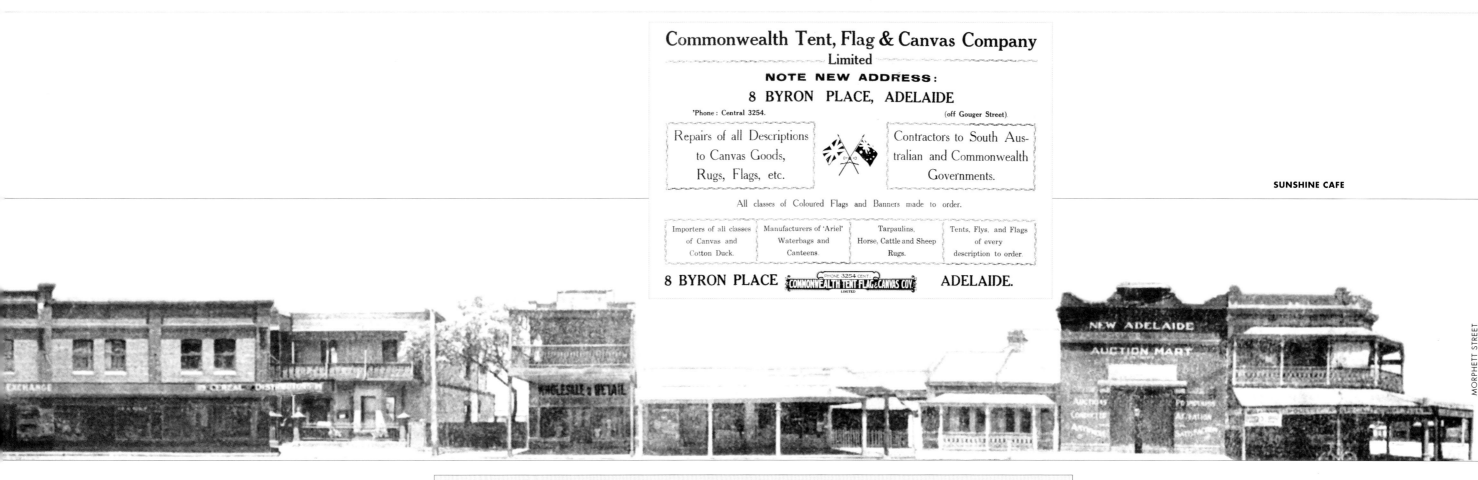

Commonwealth Tent, Flag & Canvas Company
Limited
NOTE NEW ADDRESS:
8 BYRON PLACE, ADELAIDE
'Phone: Central 3254.   (off Gouger Street)

Repairs of all Descriptions to Canvas Goods, Rugs, Flags, etc.		Contractors to South Australian and Commonwealth Governments.

All classes of Coloured Flags and Banners made to order.

Importers of all classes of Canvas and Cotton Duck.	Manufacturers of 'Ariel' Waterbags and Canteens.	Tarpaulins, Horse, Cattle and Sheep Rugs.	Tents, Flys, and Flags of every description to order.

8 BYRON PLACE   COMMONWEALTH TENT FLAG & CANVAS COY   **ADELAIDE.**

SUNSHINE CAFE

MORPHETT STREET

GOUGER STREET (SOUTH SIDE), BETWEEN FIELD STREET AND MORPHETT STREET

Unusually, Baring spared two single-storey homes along here. To the south and west were hundreds more in the city, mainly workers' cottages. This street has one of Adelaide's better reputations for recycling commercial premises into hospitality havens. But it can work the other way. In April 1953 the Sunshine Cafe on the southeast corner of Gouger and what is now Morphett Street was the scene of a triple murder, with one first-floor window escape. The killer soon was hanged at Adelaide Gaol for his crimes with a clawhammer, and the Sunshine Cafe is long gone from Gouger Street.

VICTORIA SQUARE

CITY ARCADE

"VERELLA" (Misses Gibbie and Williams), 6 City Arcade, Specialists in Children's Wear and all kinds of Crochet, Knitting, and Smocking. "CLARISSA" (Miss L. Lewis), Ladies' Hairdresser, 7 City Arcade. Guaranteed Permanent Central Waves that are permanent. Phone: C. 4595. BURGESS, Watchmaker & Jeweller, 8 City Arcade, Diamond Mounting, Wedding Rings Remodelled. Watches and Clocks cleaned and repaired. Radios. Phone: C. 3637. SUMMERFIELD, 24 City Arcade, who combines high-class work with low prices. Permanent Waves from fifteen shillings, and Resets at two shillings; Marcel Waving from one shilling. Phone: C. 5004. Ladies requiring Permanent Waves possessing a distinctive appearance visit MISS ELSIE W.A. THOMSON'S, Ladies' Hairdressers, 39 City Arcade. Permanent Waving with tongs. All classes of beauty culture. Phone: C. 2433. A.M. COOMBE, 41-42 City Arcade. A wonderful assortment of Modern Baby Prams and all classes of Wicker Work. Wicker and Sewing Machine Repairs a speciality. Phone: C. 3719. O.C. SHROWDER, 44 City Arcade, Watchmaker and Jeweller. Repairs. Wristlet Watchets, Diamond Rings, and Cut Glass. Phone: C. 291. HAROLD ROBINSON, 52 City Arcade. This old-established Shoe Store has a fine range of Boots and Shoes at prices which appeal. Phone: C. 3911. CENTRAL PROVISION STORES, City Arcade, High Class Grocers, Provision, and Tea Merchants. Phone: C. 1263.

THE MARGUERITE TOILET SALON 225a Victoria Square. Permanent Waves of lasting beauty, a speciality of this Salon. All branches of Hairdressing, Tinting, Dyeing, Trimming, Electric Head and Face Massage, are carried out by a staff of expert assistants. Chiropody, Manicure, Hot Oil Treatments, and Henna Applications are also specialised in. Phone: C. 7217

QUALITY HOUSE, 225 Victoria Square. Latest Styles in Millinery and Frocks. Phone: C. 5387.

S.O. BEILBY, Shipping and Retail Grocer and Provisions Merchant, Suburban and Country Orders. Central 5000.

ADELAIDE TAILORING CO. SA

VICTORIA SQUARE (WEST SIDE), BETWEEN CITY ARCADE AND GROTE STREET

HILTON INTERNATIONAL ADELAIDE

Under the cool verandah, Dungey the Dentist once fixed people's teeth with a cigar clenched between his own. Father and daughter ran a hat shop for ladies. At the Victoria Cafe Tom Andonis, father of Central Market fish merchant Sam Andonis, served fresh whiting. Behind them all the great butchers of Adelaide – Sainsburys, Turners, Maceys – spruiked along the glass-roofed City Arcade that stretched west from the Adelaide Tailoring shop to the Central Market. The Harcourt Gardens bus to the new suburbia stopped out the front. In the 1980s, the Hilton International took up its 99-year lease where the old shops were. In the middle of the 19th century a cathedral almost appeared in the middle of Victoria Square. After a long wait, the five-star hotel arrived on the edge instead.

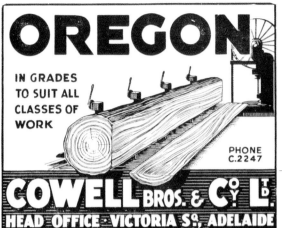

MARINE AND HARBOURS BOARD BUILDING

GEO. E. MORGAN
Marble Workers

THE ALBERT DISTRICT, No. 38, **INDEPENDENT ORDER OF RECHABITES'** Terra-Cotta-Fronted Five Storey Building, within a few yards of the General Post Office. Hall and offices to let at reasonable prices.

RECHABITE CHAMBERS (1929)

A.B.C. TOURIST BUREAU
191a Victoria Square,
Travel Information Free.
Phone: C. 8635 (2 lines).

MORIALTA CHAMBERS

WINDSOR CASTLE HOTEL

GROTE STREET

FRANKLIN STREET

VICTORIA SQUARE (WEST SIDE), BETWEEN GROTE STREET AND FRANKLIN STREET

FORMER SGIC BUILDING (1980)

FORMER MARINE AND HARBOURS BOARD BUILDING

MLC BUILDING (1957)

In 1936, the front of the Marine and Harbours Board building was 43 years short of its 34-metre roller skate due north. Now hard up against Rechabite Chambers, the migrated Italianate facade still makes passers-by blink at how Victoria Square has changed, yet hasn't. On the Franklin Street corner, the international style MLC building, or "Glass Building", was Australia's first with full glass curtain wall construction and first air-conditioned skyscraper. The modern office tower surprised Adelaide when it opened in 1957, then won the city with its rooftop weather beacon. Everyone at ground level had a how-to card: ascending flashing lights meant you were getting warmer, descending for cooler. Fast red pulses said to jump on the bus before the storm hits. The much-loved eccentric MLC beacon on what also became known as Beacon House pulsed its last the same year as the Marine and Harbours Board building moved to make way for what started life as the SGIC building.

Some time between Baring and the 1970s, buildings were removed from the southern corner of Victoria Square and Wakefield Street, and never replaced. This left pedestrians to fashion the time-honoured "goat track" path over an inner-urban vacant block. Much later it was landscaped. The open ground gives viewing space for the sandstone and bluestone St Francis Xavier Cathedral and the twin computer towers of the new green-star award-winning SA Water House, where the famous galvanised iron tram barn used to be.

Public use of Victoria Square has been a source of controversy since the day it was laid out. Keep the road link between Grote Street to the west and Wakefield Street in the east, or close it for foot traffic only? In Baring's time, the openers had it and they still do. If Victoria Square ever is resolved, life in South Australia never will be the same again. Today the square is functional; the promise of a magnificent urban space still tantalises.

VICTORIA SQUARE VIEWS

The Magistrates Court on the corner is one of the oldest buildings in the State. It is bluff and stoic, the law presenting itself heavily. To the east, the Roma Mitchell Federal Law Courts building is a carnival by comparison, with a giant peppermint Cornetto on the corner and huge Lego sets in Adelaide Football Club Crows colours for the kids.

SA WATER HOUSE   **FEDERAL LAW COURTS**   **MAGISTRATES COURT**

SUPREME COURT

The judges grumbled when they saw this building going up in 1869. The Local and Insolvency Court was so much bigger and nicer than theirs on the other side of King William Street. So the judges took it over in 1873, and the sandstone classic Supreme Court has stamped Adelaide's legal quarter at the southern end of Victoria Square ever since.

VICTORIA SQUARE, ca.1937

VICTORIA SQUARE VIEWS

ST FRANCIS XAVIER CATHEDRAL (1887)   **SA WATER HOUSE**

Sculptor John Dowie's Three Rivers fountain celebrates the Torrens, Murray and Onkaparinga rivers, valuable sources of the capital city's water supply on the planet's driest continent. Fortunately for Adelaide, the pressure on the river systems was relieved in the 21st century with the arrival of recycled water from Glenelg. Now the all–embracing Park Lands are green year round, and expected to stay that way forever. Until he became a traffic hazard, Colonel William Light still pointed the way for Adelaide from the northern end of Victoria Square. Around 1938 his statue was hauled up Montefiore Hill near Adelaide Oval, we like to think by Egyptian slaves from the Age of the Pharoahs. Hermann Baring commemorated Light's Vision after 100 years with *Progressive Adelaide*. This has been Adelaide today.

FROM THE HEART

The Adelaide of *City Streets* has been my home for 29 years, give or take a couple. One side of my street still looks much more like 1936 than 2012. We'll fight to keep it like that.

The Central Market moves closer by the day, as we learn not to drive, queue and park. It's becoming quicker to walk around the city, or take the tram, which is how it should be. Both *Progressive Adelaide* and *City Streets* were assembled mainly on foot.

The city squares, ever so slowly, come to life. Mine, Whitmore, getting on for 200 years old, is starting to show its age in the best possible way. In the later afternoon sun its big trees are dark and green and lit in gold. Yet only now is Whitmore Square being seen as a place to sit in, instead of driven around at speed and avoided.

Between these books, so to speak, levels of government flushed the people out of the square mile of Adelaide, seduced them away with quarter-acre blocks. So except for the leafy southeast corner known as the Paris end of town, and a few intransigents down the working-class southwest, or Beirut end, the street life that shapes any city decamped back then along with its inhabitants.

Now Adelaide's street life is coming back. In from the suburbs looking for a lighter, simpler life, this population spurt is made of different stuff than before. The neighbourhood now is for walking the bichon frise, not for kids' cricket under the streetlights. The urgent need of the citizens is for a cup of free trade coffee, not for a loaf of unsliced bread and a bag of potatoes.

Never will these neo-cosmopolitans live up to the likes of Ronnie the Rat,

The Doc, Chalky White, Psycho, Fluffy and the Deacon, The Italian Stallion, Lillibet, The Sewer Rat, Uncle Milty, Shinny, BP Bill and Robert of Adelaide. These legends of the original village live or have lived according to the traditions of the Beirut end for decades.

But just the same, the new wave of urbanites is challenging the city to behave like a city again, not merely as a colossal nine to five holding pen for public servants and office workers. The first thing they should be grateful for is the space they crossed to get here.

Adelaide's Park Lands are a gift, everybody's garden and place to play, precious beyond measure and the envy of other cities. Some say there's so much room, let's build a little bit on them. Which brings us to *Adelaide, so very Adelaide.*

Too much heritage, not enough development, is one argument. Too much development, not enough heritage, is the other. Either everybody thinks inside the square of the city, or nobody does. Sometimes you don't know whether to look up for progress and straight ahead for history, or vice versa.

Debate seems endless, progress allegedly stifled. *So very Adelaide.* It is both a blessing and a curse, anchored in the principle of free thinking on which South Australia was established. Which means *so very Adelaide* will never go away, and better that than the hearts of other cities deadened in haste.

As *City Streets* is published, the dream civic development of the day is along the bank of the Torrens Lake, which is Park Lands. The plan

is that people who work and live in the Adelaide of this book will adopt the revitalised precinct as their own. Outsiders will flock to it like never before in the life of South Australia.

Future readers will know the outcome, whether the city has managed to bring its heritage and its hopes together into one great people's place.

In Adelaide we still pay far too much homage to minor dignitaries, and not enough to the first residents, the Kaurna. But with the mix of past, present and future, this has been a good time to be out and about on *City Streets.*

Lance Campbell
Maxwell Street
Adelaide

▶ The early colonial settlers shifted the human focus of Adelaide from the central Victoria Square to as near as they could manage to their water supply, the River Torrens. History is likely to repeat itself over the next few years. A riverbank master development plan includes the new Festival Square plaza for the Festival Centre, still quietly proud that it beat the Sydney Opera House to the punch almost 40 years ago. Close to the site of the first Torrens crossing, a new footbridge connects the southern riverbank with Adelaide Oval and the north Parklands. Arts, sport, learning and entertainment – the things that make the City of Adelaide – will be closer kin than ever before.

PHOTO CREDITS

STATE LIBRARY OF SOUTH AUSTRALIA

Pages 2–3: Rundle Street, 1937. B 23778.

Page 11: King William Street, looking south, 1935. B 70020/11.

Page 19: King William Street – Looking from within the gates of Government House, 1936. B 7091.

Page 22: Adelaide Railway Station, 1936. B55417/252.

Page 23: 'Old Parliament House and Railway Station' – Adelaide, 1938. PRG 287/1/5/13.

Page 23: 'Parliament House in building', 1936. PRG 287/1/12/6.

Pages 30–31: North Terrace, 1928. B 4989.

Page 31: North Terrace, 1937. B 7084.

Page 31: Palais Royal, North Terrace, 1929. B 5229.

Page 32: North Terrace: North Terrace east, 1929. B 5817.

Page 32: Pulteney Street: East corner of Pulteney Street and North Terrace, Miniature Golf, 1931. B 6064.

Page 32: Crowd waiting on Pulteney Street and North Terrace for the arrival of Father Christmas, 1935. John Martin's Archive courtesy of David Jones. BRG 121/1/1625.

Pages 32–33: North Terrace, 1930. B 5699.

Page 33: North Terrace: North Terrace, east corner of Charles Street, 1934. B 6616.

Page 33: North Terrace, 1909. B 2938.

Page 33: 'Fine Stone-work – North Terrace' – Adelaide Buildings, 1936. PRG 287/1/12/28.

Page 33: North Terrace, 1929. B 5816.

Page 43: Bank Street, 1937. B 9680.

Page 44: Hindley Street, 1929. B 8493.

Page 48: Hindley Street: Wests picture theatre, Hindley Street, 1936. B 49498.

Page 66: Crowds outside the Mayfair Theatres, 1936. B 64014.

Page 68: Rundle Street, 1932. B 6200.

Page 69: Gerard and Goodman, Synagogue Place, 1928. B 4773.

Page 75: East Terrace, 1929. B 4936.

Page 77: Rundle Street, 1936. B 6907.

Page 84: Light Memorial, 1936. B 8348.

Page 85: Currie Street, 1936. B 6906.

Page 86: King William Street, 1936. B 27283.

Page 87: Currie Street, looking east, 1936. B 64049.

Page 96: Grenfell Street, 1923. B 10366.

Page 96: Grenfell Street, south side, 1935. B 6766.

Page 97: Hindmarsh Square, 1941. B 10487.

Page 98: Hindmarsh Square, 1940. B 26308.

Page 106: Waymouth Street, 1939. B 8751.

Page 109: Waymouth Street, 1937. B 6936.

Page 110: Waymouth Street, 1938. B 7375.

Page 112: Pirie Street, 1937. B 7060.

Page 113: Pirie Street, 1937. B 6944.

Page 118: Pirie Street, 1939. B 8189.

Page 119: Pirie Street, 1927. B 4319.

Page 122: Gawler Place, 1938. B 7483.

Page 123: Gawler Place, 1935. B 6785.

Page 130: Flinders Street, 1898. B 3351.

Page 130: Stow Memorial Church, 1873. B 7852.

Page 134: Fire at Dunlop Perdriau, 1940. B 7798/201.

Page 136: Flinders Street, 1929. B 8494.

Page 140: Franklin Street, 1927. B 9613.

Page 143: Grote Street, 1927. B 9593.

Page 145: Grote Street, 1927. B 9614.

Page 147: Grote Street, 1935. B 9268.

Page 150: Peoplestores, Gouger Street, 1939. B 8175.

Page 152: Moore's Department Store, Victoria Square, 1948. B 19276.

Page 153: Gouger Street, south side, 1927. B 9594.

Page 162: Victoria Square, 1937. B 60354/59.

Page 162: Victoria Square, Adelaide, 1936. PRG 287/1/12/33.

Page 163: General view of Victoria Square, 1937. B 59875.

HISTORY SA

Page 6: Floral pageant celebrating South Australia's centenary, Rundle Street, September 1936. GN09801.

Page 22: The main concourse in Adelaide Railway Station, 1935. GN05984.

Page 24: Statue of Captain Matthew Flinders, North Terrace, August 1936. GN08659.

Page 26: Floral carpet in front of the National War Memorial on North Terrace for South Australia's centenary, September 1936. GN09806.

Page 144: Corner of Grote Street and Victoria Square, showing Moore's department store, 15 September 1933. GN08637.

NEWSPIX

Page 45: Exterior of the north side of Theatre Royal building on Hindley Street, 1955. Library Advertiser, News Limited. 1265272.

ACKNOWLEDGEMENTS

SPECIAL THANKS

Paul Aikman

Michael Bollen

Vivian Bradley

John Greenshields

Liz Nicholson

Peter Verheyen

Sandy Wilkinson

THANKS

Adelaide City Council Archives

Adelaide City Council Planning Assessment Team

Advertisers in *Progressive Adelaide*

Sam Andonas

David Bailey

Graham and June Baring

Phil Broderick, History SA

Zac Campbell

Liz Caris

Nick Cawthorne

Lew Chapman

Christian Brothers College

Meagan Cox

John Davis

Lee-Ann Deer

Peter Donovan

Duke of Brunswick

Clinton Ellicott

Brenton Foster

Lavinia Gent

Steve Grieve

Sam Hill-Smith

History SA

Dieuwke Jessop, Holdfast Bay History Centre

Stephanie Johnston

Philip Jones

Reg Kyte

Margaret Ladner

Paul Limpus

Mavis Lineage

Robert Lineage

Jeff McCarthy

McDougall & Vines

Travis McLeay

Romano Manno

Jessica Marshallsay

Libby Martin

Charlotte Michalanney

Dr Peter Noblet

Philip Noblet

Mary Omond

Stephen Orr

Mandy Paul

Jo Peoples

Roger Rowse

The Salvation Army

Con Savvas

Anne-Marie Shin

Dixie Southby

State Library of South Australia

Twang Central Guitars

University of Adelaide

The Wakefield Press team

Alan Waldie

Chris Waterman

Chalky R. White

Damien Whittenbury

Carolyn Wigg

Michele Williams

Milton Wordley

MAIN SOURCES

Australian National University, National Centre of Biography, *Australian Dictionary of Biography*, adb.anu.edu.au

Cameron, Simon, *Silent Witnesses: Adelaide's Statues and Monuments*, Wakefield Press, Adelaide, 1997

Di Lernia, Nicolette and Queale, Michael, *Adelaide's Architecture and Art: a walking guide*, Wakefield Press, Adelaide, 1996

Jolly, Bridget, *Historic South West Corner*, Corporation of the City of Adelaide, 2003

Linn, Rob, *Those Turbulent Years: A History of the City of Adelaide 1929–1979*, Adelaide City Council, Historical Consultants, Adelaide, 2006

Morton, Peter, *After Light: a history of the city of Adelaide and its council, 1878–1928*, Wakefield Press, Adelaide, 1996

Murphy, Catherine, *The Market*, Wakefield Press, 2003

National Library of Australia, *Trove*, trove.nla.gov.au

State Library of South Australia, *SA Memory*, www.samemory.sa.gov.au

Venus, Richard, *Engineering a City*, Engineers Australia (SA Division), Adelaide City Council, 2009

Mick Bradley

1945–2013

This edition of *City Streets* is dedicated to Mick Bradley, master photographer and fine man.

Mick was forever on the lookout for poetic moments in everyday life. He spent more than a year around Adelaide shooting its city streets. Then, along with Lance Campbell, he spent more than another year taking *City Streets* to its readership. As befits a musician as well as a photographer, Mick was a natural performer with people. He was a one-off, kind and very talented. Mick's smile was infectious. He lit up a room, and a day.

Mick Bradley died unexpectedly aged just 68. He is sadly missed and fondly remembered by his adored wife Vivian, his children and grandchildren, his large extended family, and his many friends around the world. We are poorer for his absence, richer for his life.

Photograph by Daryl Austin

Wakefield Press is an independent publishing and
distribution company based in Adelaide, South Australia.
We love good stories and publish beautiful books.
To see our full range of books, please visit our website at
www.wakefieldpress.com.au
where all titles are available for purchase.

Find us!

Twitter: www.twitter.com/wakefieldpress
Facebook: www.facebook.com/wakefield.press
Instagram: instagram.com/wakefieldpress

DRIVE-YOURSELF CARS

Late Model
SEDANS AND COUPES
for Hire

GUARANTEED SERVICE

CARAVANS FOR HIRE
AND BUILT TO ORDER.

VISITORS AND TRAVELLERS
ESPECIALLY CATERED FOR

HIRE CAR AND CARAVAN ON TOUR

INTERIOR OF FOUR BERTH TOURING CARAVAN

Phone
C 7286

BEST'S HIRE SERVICE

375 King William Street
Adelaide

Hand Coloured
Christmas Stationery
Greeting Cards
Calendars, Etc.

TYPEWRITING

Illustrated
Stencil Drawings
Music Copies, Etc.
Fancy Note Papers

E. IRENE VINEY

GRENFELL BUILDING

55 GRENFELL STREET

ADELAIDE

Telephone: Central 88

MULTIGRAPHING

DUPLICATING

FOOT SPECIALIST

Miss Blanche Jackson

Hair, Skin, and
Foot Specialist

Only Address:

Gawler Chambers
North Terrace
Adelaide

Painless Treatments
for all Foot Troubles.

All Instruments
Thoroughly
Sterilized

CONSULTATIONS
FREE

'Phone: C. 4166

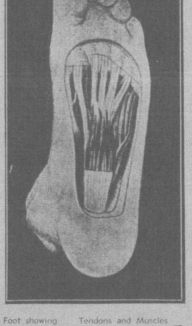

Foot showing   Tendons and Muscles

This is our Striking Sign :

BARING PRINTERS

10 Chesser Street, Adelaide.

WHEN BUSINESS SLACKENS!

Phone
c 2392 **Les. J. Kyte**

ADVERTISING PRACTITIONER AND COUNSELLOR
MARKET SURVEYOR, &c.—QUALIFIED BY DIPLOMA
10 CHESSER STREET ———— ADELAIDE